J. SUTHERLAND
ADRESS

J BRADSHAW
102 COAL PARK
DLNESS
IVIFORV

BUILD YOUR OWN

OFF-ROAD BUGGY

FOR AS LITTLE AS £100

BUILD YOUR OWN
OFF-ROAD BUGGY
FOR AS LITTLE AS £100

RON CHAMPION

First published in March 2002
Reprinted September 2002
Reprinted 2004 (twice)

A catalogue record for this book is available from the British Library.

ISBN 1 85960 642 3

Library of Congress catalog card no. 2001132567

Published by Haynes Publishing, Sparkford, Yeovil, Somerset BA22 7JJ, UK
Tel: 01963 442030 Fax: 01963 440001
Int. tel: +44 1963 442030 Fax: +44 1963 440001
E-mail: sales@haynes.co.uk
Website: www.haynes.co.uk

Haynes North America Inc., 861 Lawrence Drive, Newbury Park, California 91320, USA

Printed and bound in Britain by J.H. Haynes & Co. Ltd, Sparkford

Contents

Dedication

This book is dedicated to the memory of my mother, Ann Elizabeth Champion, who passed away in the Autumn of 2000. Having seen the early photographs of the Buggy she unfortunately did not live to see the project completed, nor to have the opportunity to have a go, which, even at the age of 77, I am sure she would have done. The spirit of adventure and enthusiasm is in the soul and should not be discouraged. I hope that having read this book, like my old Mum, it inspires you to have a go.

Acknowledgements

I would like to acknowledge the assistance of those who have helped to make this book a reality.

First and foremost I would like to thank Rory Perrett for his contribution, especially in the preparation of the manuscript and the drawings used in the book, and without whom it might never have been completed.

I would also like to thank Steve Williams for the taking the photographs, and Gordon Gilbert for producing the original 3D CAD drawing of the Buggy's frame. Thanks also to John Hardaker who produced the line drawings in their finished form, and to front cover model Karen Thurston.

I would like to thank Justin Cole of Racers Hardware, Crowland for his technical expertise, the use of facilities and the support from all his staff, especially Colin and Trudi, and a big thank-you to Derek Manders for trying out my manuscript to see if you really could build a Buggy from it.

Finally, I would like to thank my wife, Mary, for supporting me in the writing of another book.

Introduction

When you're the son of a car-mad engineer you really don't stand a chance! James, who like me grew up surrounded by cars, parts of cars, tools, oil, etc, was one of those sons. Now, twenty or so years on, he's a driver in the successful Locost car race series for cars built to the design appearing in the book I wrote in 1996. The first Locost car was built for James, and since the book *Build Your Own Sports Car For As Little As £250* was published, thousands of other people have been able to enjoy building their own car. However, the Locost wasn't the first vehicle to be built for James!

James always liked going with me to the local dump, an event that usually resulted in us returning with more than we took. On one occasion, when he was about four years old, we found a small commercially built go-kart, which had a steel chassis, 1½in-wide pump-up tyres on wire wheels, and was propelled, like a bicycle, with pedals connected by a chain to the back axle. The kart was missing only the seat and the steering wheel, and the rest of the weekend was spent getting this contraption into working order. Another trip to the dump secured a plastic seat from a stacking chair, and a steering wheel was found and secured to the steering column. For the next few weeks James had a great time peddling his 'car' round and round the garden, until he decided that the effort of peddling was too much like hard work.

As I'm the type of person who never throws anything away – the trips to the dump were always to dispose of my wife's junk – I had a

search in the shed and the garage to see what I could come up with to motorise the kart. It was decided that the starter motor from a Mini car would provide power, and that the manually operated starter solenoid switch from a Morris Minor would be the 'go' switch. A Suffolk Colt lawnmower gave up its smallest 8-toothed sprocket, which was brazed to the shaft of the starter motor once the Bendix gear mechanism had been removed. A few cables, an old car

The author gives two new drivers tips on how to handle the prototype Buggy. (Steve Williams)

battery and a couple of hours work later, James was the proud owner of his own self-propelled vehicle. We did have one or two teething problems; I prefer to call it 'R and D'! The power delivery to the back wheels was instantaneous, with James's head being jerked violently backwards every time he pressed the 'go' switch, and lots of wheelspin due to the tyres having to act as a clutch. Great fun for James, but of great concern to his mother, not only because of the grooves appearing across the lawn, but also because of the damage it could be doing to her precious son's brain as his head was thrown around. On the technical front, the biggest problem was that the kart wouldn't steer. The solid axle driving the two rear wheels wanted to propel the vehicle forwards in a straight line, regardless of whether the front wheels were pointing to the left or to the right.

The following weekend I was back out in the workshop salvaging some more sprockets from the Suffolk Colt. Using the new sprockets, together with some lengths of chain, we built a reduction gearbox. This not only reduced the torque and lowered the top speed, but also virtually eliminated the wheelspin, making the whole vehicle a lot more usable. An additional bonus was that because the kart now had several chain runs there was a delay between the solenoid being operated and the drive fully taking up the slack in the chains, which in turn saved the strain on James's neck. We solved the steering problem by having only one of the rear wheels on the rear axle driven, leaving the other free to rotate, creating a sort of crude differential.

Braking was provided by a hand-brake that operated directly on the rear tyres, but we were also pleased to find that as soon as the power was switched off the motor became a very effective brake. I did have thoughts of regenerative braking using complicated switchgear to recharge the battery!

James used the kart regularly for the next few years until he got his first motorcycle at the age of seven. The electric kart was passed onto a French family and is still being used by the next generation of youngsters.

After playing around with the kart, I got into motorcycle-engined buggies when I was involved in youth and community work, and came up with a basic design not dissimilar to the one in this book. Young people in a youth training workshop who recycled the major components from scrap motorcycles successfully built dozens of these buggies.

After building the prototype Buggy which appears in this book, and having written the first draft of this book, I decided that it would be a good idea to see if it was, in fact, possible for someone to build a Buggy using my instructions! A willing volunteer was found in the shape of Derek Manders, an old friend who had successfully built a

The prototype Buggy in action. (Steve Williams)

Derek Manders's granddaughter, Charlotte, at the wheel of his Buggy. (Derek Manders)

Locost using my first book, *Build Your Own Sports Car For As Little As £250.* Having heard about the Buggy project, Derek decided that he would like to build one for his granddaughter, Charlotte. So, armed with a copy of the original manuscript for this book, some photographs of the building of the prototype Buggy, and a complete welded Buggy frame, we sent him off to see what he could do. Derek's brief was to incorporate his own ideas and build his own variation on the Buggy concept, on the understanding that as long as he didn't alter the frame from the standard one supplied, the rest was up to him. You'll find that I have included some of Derek's alternative solutions to the Buggy build as 'Alternative solutions' sidebars in this book, just to reinforce the message that I've described one way to build a Buggy, but it's not the only way. The book shows the basic design and is intended to get you started and to get you thinking. Skilled engineers might wish to modify the design, but my advice is to stay small and simple. If the design is varied, seek the advice of a competent engineer or someone experienced with off-road vehicles. The original design is thoroughly tried and tested.

Chapter 1

Skills required

I've found that enthusiasm breeds skills, and during my many years as an engineering instructor I've seen time and again that if someone really wants to do something, they find that, with application, they *can* do it. Since you've bought this book, though, I assume it's more likely than not that you already have some basic mechanical skill and knowledge. If this isn't the case, all is not lost, as there are several ways (formally and informally) to acquire the skills you will need.

First and foremost, in building your Buggy on a minimal budget, the most important skill you're going to need is patience, as it will take time to source the materials and parts, and build everything yourself. Patience is also an essential aspect of learning to weld.

WELDING

The most important equipment for joining metal is a welder, and the most important skill is knowing how to use it. This is a skill you can teach yourself from instruction books and by practising on metal scrap, though most will benefit from professional tuition. Equipment suppliers are generally prepared to give basic instruction to new purchasers of welding equipment.

There are also several training centres specialising in welding, and most technical colleges and further education institutes offer evening classes in all types of welding and metal fabrication.

Booklets containing useful information on equipment and safety procedures can be obtained from the British Oxygen Company (BOC) Group, and that company also produces a range of training videos. (Contact BOC Gases, The Priestley Centre, 10 Priestley Road, Surrey Research Park, Guildford, Surrey GU2 5XY. Phone: 01483 579857.)

When buying second-hand, be sure that the vendor gives you a satisfactory demonstration of the equipment in use. He may also be prepared to give you some basic instruction as well.

Even if you already have experience of welding, it's essential to familiarise yourself with the equipment and materials you will be using. I've been welding for over 30 years, but when using an unfamiliar welding set I always try a test weld on a piece of scrap, preferably an offcut from the material I am about to use. It would be a good idea to make up a rectangle or a cube from the tube you will be using to make the frame of your Buggy, and keep practising until your joints are perfect.

Welding equipment available to the home builder is likely to be one of 3 main types, gas (oxy-acetylene), MIG (metal inert gas) and arc.

Metal cleaning

Whatever type of welding you use, the pieces of metal to be welded must be free from rust and clean. The cleaner the metal, the better the joint. Good wire brushes, emery cloth and wire wool will help you clean up your joints both before and after welding.

Gas welding

This is traditional oxy-acetylene welding, a method developed by the French at the beginning of the century using the two gases oxygen and acetylene. The advantage is that this method does not need a supply of electricity, so it can be used anywhere. The main supplier of oxy-acetylene equipment in the UK is the BOC Group, and while you can purchase torches, hoses and gauges, the gas cylinders can only be rented. Ideal for small jobs is the BOC Portapak.

It's vitally important to follow the correct safety procedures when using pressurised cylinders, and for new users this needs to become a habit from the beginning. Gas cylinders are colour coded – acetylene cylinders are maroon and oxygen cylinders are black. Acetylene smells of garlic and burns with a smoky yellow-orange flame, but when correctly mixed with oxygen an incredibly hot flame is produced.

Make sure the equipment you are using is fitted with flashback arresters to prevent flames travelling back into the cylinders. Pressure regulators are screwed into the cylinder valves – in the case of acetylene cylinders a left-hand thread is used, and for oxygen cylinders it's a right-hand thread. The hoses connecting the pressure regulators to the torch are red for acetylene and blue for oxygen. Check that the hoses are of best quality and in good condition (do not use them if there are signs of wear), and have hose check valves fitted.

Always keep gas welding equipment free from oil and grease, follow the supplier's instructions when assembling and, when assembled, check for leaks. I use a cup of soapy water and a paint brush to brush water over the joints. If there are any leaks, they will show as bubbles. If you do detect a leak it can quite often be cured by a further 'nip' with a spanner, but if this doesn't work and you are quite sure all the threads were clean, do not tamper with it – take the cylinder back to the supplier and have it checked. Do not over tighten any of the joints as most of the fittings are made of brass and the threads are easy to strip.

Before you get started be sure that your work area is free from any combustible material, such as oily rags, fuel tanks etc, and that it is well ventilated. See also that your cylinders are secured in an upright position (preferably chained on a trolley), and wear the correct welding goggles and gloves. Having familiarised yourself with the operating instructions and set the gas pressures for the steel thickness you are going to work on (all shown in the BOC booklet), open the acetylene valve and light your torch with the spark igniter. Adjust the acetylene flame until the smoke just disappears, then open the oxygen valve until you achieve a clearly defined very light blue central flame. This central flame will be surrounded by a darker blue outer flame which shows you are using equal amounts of both gases. This is known as a neutral flame – ideal for welding steel.

If you're right-handed, hold the welding rod in your left hand and start on the right-hand side of the joint to be welded. If you're left-handed, hold the welding rod in your right hand and start on the left side of the joint. Bring the flame to a little over 1/8in from the joint, and hold the nozzle at about 70 degrees. Through your goggles you will see the steel turn into a

Fig. 1.1. Gas welding equipment. The taller cylinder contains oxygen, the shorter one acetylene. Suitable protective clothing, dark goggles or a mask and thick gloves should be worn when welding. (Steve Williams)

molten pool. The welding rod tip is introduced into the molten steel where it will also melt and mix. You then move the flame along the joint, allowing the molten pool and welding rod to mix as you go.

Although it will take some time to fully master the art of oxy-acetylene welding your frame, once you have done so it is a satisfying though slow process.

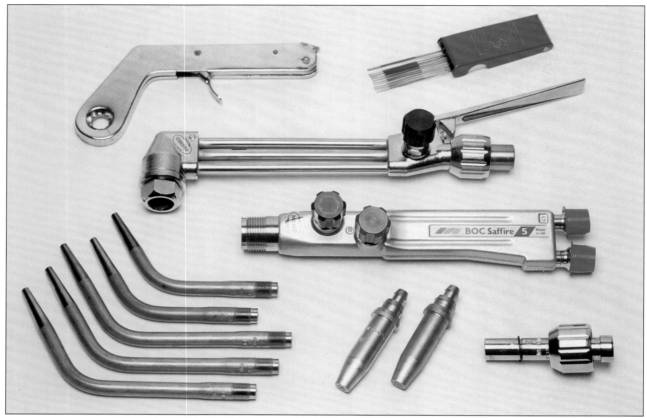

Fig. 1.2. A spark gun, set of nozzle cleaners, a torch, mixer and welding and cutting nozzles for a gas welder. (Steve Williams)

Mig welding

MIG (metal inert gas) welding is, in my opinion, the best method for welding your frame and other parts that need to be fabricated. I've instructed many people in this skill, and my student success rate has been 100 per cent. My usual method is to give direct one-to-one instruction for 30 minutes, familiarising the student with the controls and the techniques. I then give them a quiet work area with the MIG equipment, a big box of steel offcuts of all shapes and thicknesses, and leave them to practise. I check his or her progress from time to time during the day, advising and demonstrating as necessary, and by the end of the day everyone, without exception so far, has been sufficiently competent to weld a frame. By the time the frame is finished, they should be skilled and confident

enough to fabricate brackets and all the other welded components required. I firmly believe that with the set of instructions provided with a new MIG welder, a person can teach himself/herself to MIG weld. The availability of small, low-priced MIG welding equipment has brought welding well within the scope of the DIY enthusiast.

Small MIG welders are available from some car accessory shops and tool shops, and the throwaway gas cylinders involved can be purchased over the counter for just a few pounds. Hiring is an alternative, and if you have your frame tubes already cut to length it should be possible to fabricate the frame over a weekend, thereby keeping hire costs to a minimum.

All welding is basically the same, but with a MIG welder you need an electric power supply. The equipment's controls should be set according to the instructions, but

basically you have the power (or amperage) set low for thin steel and high for thick steel. The welding wire is on a spool or drum, and is fed through a tube to a nozzle which is held close to the joint to be welded. When you squeeze the trigger on the handgrip it activates a motor which feeds the wire through the nozzle to the joint. The material to be welded is attached to the welding equipment by an earth lead, so as soon as the wire touches the material it completes the circuit causing an electric arc. The wire and two pieces of metal to be joined immediately melt into a small pool and fuse together. Whilst this is happening, gas (either carbon dioxide or a carbon dioxide/argon mix – both being inert gases) from the cylinder attached to the machine also flows from the nozzle under pressure to surround the weld area, excluding

Fig. 1.3. A portable MIG welder. Remember you must wear a full-face shield to protect you from the ultraviolet light given off, and thick gloves should be used to stop your hands getting burnt. (Steve Williams)

any impurities from the immediate atmosphere and cooling the weld area. If you let go of the trigger, the arc, wire and gas flow stop, ready to be restarted by squeezing the trigger again. The arcing creates a very bright light, so your eyes must be protected by a special face mask. This mask will also protect your face from the ultraviolet light given off. The effects are rather like sun burn, so protect your hands with thick gloves, and also protect any other exposed skin. Keep children and animals well away, and if you have helpers or observers, provide them with face masks, too.

The only time I have experienced problems with MIG welding is when working outside in windy conditions, when poor welds can result because the gas shield is blown away. You can overcome this to some extent by turning up the gas pressure or, if that fails, by making a windbreak – sometimes just standing a box, or the welder itself on the windy side is enough.

Arc welding

Although small arc welders are very cheap to buy or hire, it takes a long time to develop the necessary skills (though not as long as with gas welding) and it is not really suitable for thin steel. The 16swg (standard wire gauge) tubes for your frame are about as thin as you can go with an arc welder, and whilst an experienced welder would make a good strong job of it, an inexperienced welder could well have difficulty with such thin material, and I would not recommend welding your frame as a first job. However, it is not impossible – but remember what I said about the need for patience.

Arc welding is not unlike MIG welding, as both use an electric arc to melt the metal to be joined, but instead of a continuous spool of wire, the arc welder uses rods, and instead of gas the rods are coated in a special flux which melts with the rod. When the weld has cooled, the flux remains on the surface and needs to be chipped away with a special pointed hammer (a chipping hammer) to expose what, it is hoped, is a good weld beneath.

SAFETY PRECAUTIONS WHEN WELDING

● **Keep the area clear of combustible material.**
● **Always wear the correct eye protection.**
● **Wear strong boots and gloves, and thick overalls to protect yourself against sparks.**
● **Keep a suitable fire extinguisher close by.**
● **Do not allow electric welding sets to become wet or damp.**
● **Weld in a well-ventilated area and avoid breathing in fumes.**
● **Keep children and pets away from the work area.**
● **Keep oil and grease away from oxy-acetylene equipment.**
● **Keep gas cylinders upright and secured.**
● **Always turn off the gas supply and mains electricity when not in use.**

Fig. 1.4. Painting – two coats of grey primer and two coats of gloss paint will give a smart and durable finish which is easily touched up if damaged and, best of all, is cheap. (Steve Williams)

ENGINEERING SKILLS

If you've selected your donor motorcycle well, you should have no need to get into rebuilding the engine or gearbox, but you will have to overhaul and bleed the brakes, and fit brake pipes, etc. All the information you need will be in the *Haynes Service and Repair Manual* for your motorcycle, but you may like to back up this knowledge with evening classes at your local technical college or by joining a local motor or motorcycle club where you will find like-minded people who might well be interested in your project, and who may be able to help with knowledge, skills, practical help and even the loan of tools and equipment.

PAINTING

When the frame is complete it can be brush painted. Although I can spray paint, I still brush paint the frame, mainly because spraying a tubular frame is so wasteful of paint – there are more 'holes' than tubes.

As an alternative to painting, you may decide to have the frame powder-coated. This process will have to be carried out by a powder-coating specialist, and if you're not too fussy about the colour your frame ends up, you should be able to get a good price by having your frame coated at the same time as another batch of components.

Chapter 2
Tools, equipment and workshop safety

This Chapter lists all the tools and equipment required to build your Buggy. I'm acutely aware that we are producing a budget Buggy, and that the cost of the tools and equipment could exceed the cost of the finished project, but you'll probably have most of these tools already, or possibly you can borrow or hire them.

Included are several tools which, although not essential, will certainly enable you to tackle certain things more quickly and easily.

If you have to purchase tools, my advice is to buy the best you can afford, whether new or second-hand. If you look after them they will last a lifetime. Indeed, a large proportion of my hand tools belonged to my father and father-in-law. Remember, the best are not necessarily new. In fact, most of my metalworking tools and measuring tools have been purchased second-hand for just a few pounds, and I would not have got more effective or accurate tools had I bought them new.

BUYING TOOLS

Most large towns these days have hire shops, and I think it's worth considering hiring power tools or welding equipment if you do not already have them, but for small hand tools it's best to purchase your own, particularly if you can find good second-hand examples.

Car boot sales and autojumbles are the best source of second-hand tools and equipment. At these places it's expected of you to haggle, which is all part of the fun.

Advertisements in local papers are also quite good for second-hand bargains. I've found not only tools, but also wheels, engines and complete donor motorcycles through such ads. One person I know who built his own car, bought a second-hand MIG welder, built his car, then sold the welder for a profit – that's enterprise for you!

The most important advice I can give you is to take your time collecting tools, equipment, materials and parts. There have been times when I've spent weeks looking for that elusive item, then after having purchased it new, a similar one has turned up at a fraction of the price I paid. So, remember, more haste – less cash saved!

To build the frame of your Buggy you're going to need some basic hand tools for measuring, cutting and shaping your frame tubes, and a welder for joining them together. Beyond that, you'll probably already have most of the basic tools required to build your Buggy. The following information will help you to decide whether you need to obtain any extra tools.

TOOLS REQUIRED

A very basic toolkit would comprise:

Basic hand tools

Socket set
Set of ring spanners
Set of open-ended spanners
Set of Allen keys
A small selection of screwdrivers

A selection of pliers/wire cutters
A selection of clamps
Large and small hammers
Steel tape measure
Steel ruler and set square
Hacksaw
Files – one flat, one round
Wire brush
Cold chisels and centre punch

Essential power tools

Electric drill with a selection of drill bits
Welding set

Bench tools

Vice (a Record No. 5 or 6, for example)
Bench drill

Specialist tools

The following specialist tools will be required to complete your Buggy, but as they will be used for a relatively small amount of work, you may wish to farm the work out to a helpful friend, a suitably equipped garage or a local engineering workshop. They will probably be only too glad to help when you tell them about your Buggy project.

Brake pipe flaring tool
Metalworking lathe
Tank/hole saw or jigsaw

Your Buggy can be built with just the previously mentioned tools plus a few basic household items such as scissors for cutting out card patterns, etc, and a pencil or a piece of chalk for marking out.

With regard to hand files, I

Fig. 2.1. A good quality set of sockets and spanners will last a lifetime. A selection of different lengths of socket-set extension is useful. Keeping your sockets on bars, as shown, will make it easier to select them for use and prevent them becoming lost. (Steve Williams)

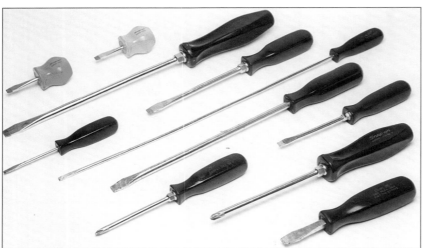

Fig. 2.2. A useful selection of screwdrivers. (Steve Williams)

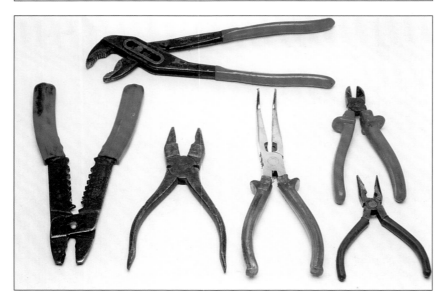

Fig. 2.3. A selection of pliers, including wire strippers and wire cutters. (Steve Williams)

Fig. 2.4. Wire brushes. (Steve Williams)

Fig. 2.5. Chisels and punches. Ensure that chisels and punches are kept sharp for accurate marking and punching. (Steve Williams)

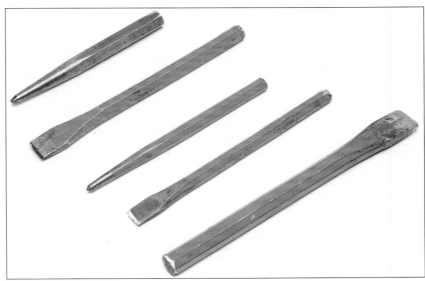

would be the first to admit that an angle grinder could speed up the job considerably, as it can remove as much unwanted metal in a minute as a hand file can in an hour, but when keeping to a tight budget we have to remember that elbow grease is free.

Measuring and marking

A tape measure, a ruler and a set square are the most basic tools of metal working. Anything you produce without these will not be accurate. For workshop use, and particularly metalworking, you

really need a steel tape measure and a metal rule, as plastic or wooden ones will soon become damaged and broken.

The ruler I use most of all is made of steel, one yard (around one metre) long, and only cost me a few pence years ago from a market stall selling second-hand tools. With some fine wire wool, rust was quickly removed and it has been used almost daily ever since. A small 6in steel ruler, $\frac{1}{2}$in wide, is useful for work in restricted places.

A 10ft (3m) retractable steel tape measure is very handy to have – it helps you measure around curves

and it fits neatly in your pocket for those trips to scrapyards, etc.

Set squares come in a variety of types and sizes, the only one I had for many years was a 12in x 6in (305mm x 152mm) carpenter's square, and this was used to build several space-frame chassis most accurately. I subsequently acquired a 24in x 18in (600mm x 450mm) roofing square which is proving invaluable for marking out larger areas. A combination square is a useful tool as it comes with a protractor head for measuring angles, and it also has a spirit level incorporated. If I've been away from my home workshop I've often

Fig. 2.6. Measuring equipment. A roofer's set square, a retractable steel tape measure, a carpenter's set square, a combination square and a 24in steel ruler. (Steve Williams)

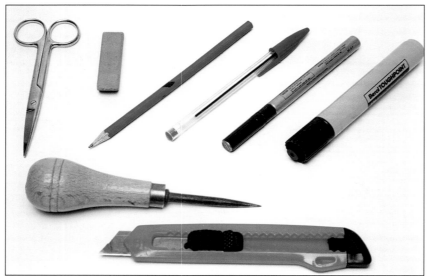

Fig. 2.7. Cutting and marking tools for cardboard templates, etc. (Steve Williams)

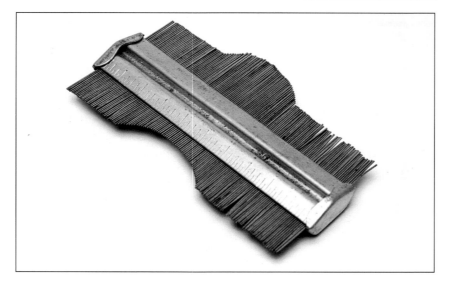

Fig. 2.8. A profile gauge. (Steve Williams)

improvised and checked squareness with one edge of a notebook, or have made a quick triangle with an offcut of steel or aluminium sheet.

A centre punch is needed to mark metal for drilling holes. It makes a small indentation when struck with a hammer – essential to centralise the drill bit. The indentation holds the tip of the drill bit in position and stops it skidding and skipping across your workpiece as you start the drill.

You'll need a scriber for marking out metal, and one can be made from a broken or old screwdriver by grinding or filing the end to a point.

Something of a luxury is a profile gauge. These can be expensive new, but again can be purchased second-hand. They're particularly useful when working with round tube, and will help to give the correct profile of joints and brackets, etc, which are to be fitted to the tubes.

Cutting and shaping

A good quality hacksaw with a sturdy frame is essential, and it's worthwhile purchasing good quality blades – a quality blade will make the job quicker and will last longer. Take advice when purchasing blades, and always fit them so that the cutting teeth face the front, so that the blade cuts on the forward stroke. A wire-frame 'junior' hacksaw is ideal for tight areas or small jobs.

Files are used to give a smooth finish, or for shaping, by removing metal. They come in various lengths and shapes. The shape is the file's cross-section, which can be flat, square, triangular, round or half round. The teeth can be coarse or fine, or anything in between. A coarse or 'bastard-cut' file will remove a lot of metal quickly but will leave a rough finish. A 'second-cut' file will remove metal slowly and leave a smooth finish. The finest finish is achieved with a 'smooth-cut' file. The pointed end

of the file is called the tang, to which is fixed a handle which always used to be wooden but is now quite often plastic. **Never use a file without a handle** or you are sure to have an accident.

Clamping

Clamps come in a variety of types, but all serve the same function of gripping two or more pieces of material together. The most common type is the G-clamp on which one adjustable face is moved by a screw thread. There are also lever-locking clamps which come in several designs and sizes. The specialist ones tend to be a little expensive, but I've found that I can make my own by buying locking clamps with worn out jaws, then making my own jaws from scrap and welding them on. In this

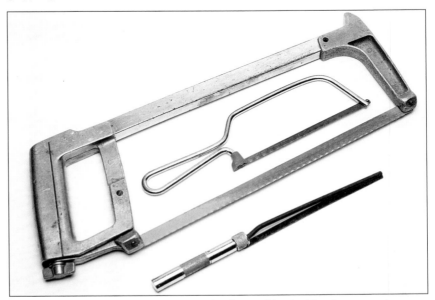

Fig. 2.9. Metal-cutting saws. Large hacksaw, 'Junior' hacksaw, and a very useful handle for holding a 'Junior' hacksaw blade when sawing in tight corners. (Steve Williams)

Fig. 2.10. A selection of files. It is essential that a correctly fitting handle is used at all times. (Steve Williams)

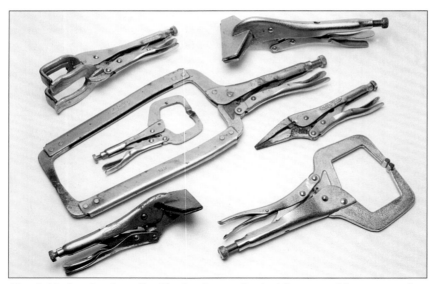

Fig. 2.11. A selection of self-grip clamps for holding metal items together when welding. (Steve Williams)

Fig. 2.12. A battery-operated rechargeable drill. Not essential if you have a mains-operated drill, but so light and compact to use. (Steve Williams)

way you can obtain a full set of specialist welding clamps for a fraction of their cost new.

The ideal vice for work on your Buggy project will have 5in (127mm) wide jaws. It will hold work safely when you're cutting, drilling, grinding and filing. You can also use it for clamping two pieces of metal together when welding, but remember not to let the heat get too close to the vice as this could damage it. Secure your vice firmly, and remember that a vice is only as secure as the bench it's bolted to.

Drilling and grinding

An electric drill is the one power tool that's almost indispensable. Apart from making holes it can be used to power grinding stones,

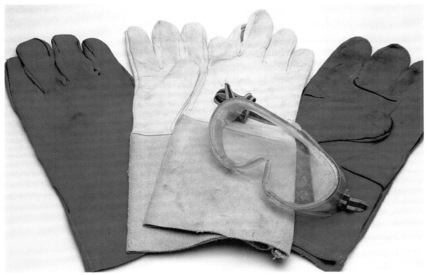

Fig. 2.13. Gauntlets and goggles. Essential for grinding and cutting operations. (Steve Williams)

rotary wire brushes and various types of sanding and buffing accessories **(and don't forget to wear goggles when using it for these purposes)**.

A note of caution: if buying this tool second-hand, please have it checked over by a qualified electrician. If the cable is frayed or damaged, or the plug wired incorrectly, the results can be fatal.

If you do acquire an angle grinder it will probably be the most potentially dangerous tool in your kit and, as with the drill, if buying second-hand, do have it checked by a qualified electrician and **always wear goggles and protective clothing (including strong gloves and ear defenders or plugs) when using an angle grinder.** The three main attachments for it are grinding discs, cutting discs and sanding discs which are used in conjunction with a flexible plastic backing. Used with care, an angle grinder will save hours of work and will produce a professional finish to your metal.

Welding equipment

As explained in Chapter 1, there are three main methods of welding – gas, MIG and arc. I would advise

a beginner to obtain MIG welding equipment for two main reasons. The first is cost, as nowadays inexpensive DIY MIG welders are available both new and second-hand. The materials are inexpensive too, and – perhaps most important – with MIG a novice welder can produce first class results with minimal training.

An arc welder is cheaper to buy, but more difficult to master, especially on the material used to construct the Buggy. The welding is more violent, less easy to control and more inclined to burn through or blow holes in the workpiece. Another problem is that the welds form a black slag which has to be chipped away with a special pointed hammer, making it a messy and time-consuming process.

The other of the three methods is gas welding, involving two gas cylinders, one of oxygen and one of acetylene, together with hoses, gauges, torch and a welding or bottle trolley. This is probably the most versatile equipment of all, as it can be used for heating and cutting (useful for dismantling your donor motorcycle, as a little heat will release the most stubborn rusted nuts), bending and shaping, welding and brazing. But I have found that it takes longer to teach

novices to gas weld, and certainly a greater level of skill is required than in MIG welding. It's also slower and, because of the greater amount of local heat generated, one of the major problems is heat distortion, which could affect the accuracy of your Buggy frame. Having said all that, the neatness of gas welding done by an expert is a joy to behold. It is not possible to purchase the gas cylinders outright. Instead, you have to enter into a rental agreement with the supplier, but it is possible to rent miniature cylinders (BOC Portapak). Although not aimed specifically at the novice or DIY market, they might help reduce costs and storage space. I think it would be fair to say, though, that this type of equipment is potentially more dangerous than other forms of welding.

WORKSHOP SAFETY

This is so important that I could fill a book just listing all the dangers and things to be aware of, but basically safety is down to just plain common sense. Think of your own safety, think of others, and think the job through before you start.

Every effort must be made to ensure a high standard of workmanship when building your Buggy. If in doubt, the author cannot recommend highly enough that you seek advice from a professional engineer or welder. At all times, work safely and with due consideration for others.

Power tools and welding equipment present the greatest hazards. Make sure that all your electrical equipment is safe (including extension leads), and if in doubt have it checked by a qualified electrician. Flying sparks from angle grinders and swarf from drilling can cause terrible eye injuries. When using any grinding, drilling, buffing, polishing, cutting or shaping power tools, wear safety goggles. Make sure the goggles are in good condition. If you can't see what you're doing and are working part blind, it produces yet another hazard. Make sure you have goggles for helpers and spectators, as sparks can travel up to 20ft (6m). For welding, have an adequate mask or goggles, and be aware that gas welding goggles are for gas welding and not for MIG or arc welding. For these you use full-face masks. For any welding, wear protective clothing and gloves, making sure your arms are well covered. Keep all inflammable substances away from the workshop where you are welding or grinding.

Keep a clean and tidy workspace, and avoid trailing leads and cables, as these constitute tripping hazards.

As your Buggy frame takes shape it will need supporting at a safe and comfortable working height. Axle stands are ideal, but I also have several 18in (50cm) square wooden blocks which make firm supports. Do not be tempted to balance the project on bricks or boxes, as these may crumble or collapse.

Always keep a basic first-aid kit close by, and make sure other people know where it is. It also makes sense to have a fire extinguisher in your work area. One of the dry powder type suitable for electrical and liquid fires is ideal.

Ensure that there are no flammable liquids or materials stored in the workshop such as paint thinners etc. Remember most accidents can be avoided using common sense.

See also the welding safety precautions listed in Chapter 1.

Do's and Don'ts

● **DO** read this book from start to finish before starting the project.
● **DO** ensure that your welding is up to standard before starting work.
● **DO** purchase a first-aid kit and keep it in your work area.
● **DO** wear proper protective overalls, footwear, gloves and safety goggles when appropriate.
● **DO** get someone to check periodically that all is well when working alone in the workshop.
● **DO** keep loose clothing and long hair well out of the way of moving mechanical parts.
● **DO** seek professional advice if in doubt about safety related matters like brake and steering components.
● **DO** ensure that when working on the Buggy frame, the frame is supported securely on axle or chassis stands.
● **DO** ensure that all extension leads and cables on any power equipment are sound and free from cuts and damage, and check that the correct fuse is fitted.
● **DO** keep your work area neat and tidy, with no tripping hazards.
● **DO** mop up oil and fuel spills at once.
● **DON'T** smoke or allow naked lights (including pilot lights) anywhere near petrol or petrol vapour. Also beware of creating sparks (electrically or by the use of tools).
● **DON'T** weld without a fire extinguisher close by.
● **DON'T** weld without using an approved welding mask or welding goggles.
● **DON'T** work under vehicles supported by jacks, bricks, breeze blocks, etc.
● **DON'T** allow any inflammable substances to be stored in the workshop where you are welding or grinding, and this includes oily rags.
● **DON'T** use ill-fitting tools which may slip and cause injury.
● **DON'T** allow children or pets to play in or near a vehicle being worked on.

Chapter 3
Sourcing what you need

I developed the original concept of the Buggy when I was a school teacher and part-time youth worker, and variations were made on the theme in school and in various youth clubs. As such, this design is ideally suited for young people from the age of eight to sixteen. The whole philosophy behind the design and construction of the Buggy is to keep it safe, simple and cheap.

This book describes one way to build a Buggy, but it's not the only way. The book shows the basic design and is intended to get you started and to get you thinking. Skilled engineers might wish to modify the design, but my advice is to stay small and simple. If the design is varied, seek the advice of a competent engineer or someone experienced with off-road vehicles. The original design is tried and tested.

THE ORIGINAL BUGGY DESIGN

My original intention was to use a small-capacity engine such as the Honda 50 or 70. The advantage of an engine such as this is that it is still plentiful, cheap, has a centrifugal clutch and, therefore, two-pedal operation (go and stop). But, young people being what they are, there is always a temptation to fit larger and larger engines.

I feel that the maximum engine size safe for this design is 250cc, and even then one disc brake on the rear axle is starting to become overworked. It would be a simple matter to fit twin discs and calipers, but the real answer for a high-

capacity engine would be front disc brakes. If anyone wishes to explore this route further, there are various publications available aimed at kart racers, and suitable equipment is readily available, both new and second-hand.

The original Buggy described in this book was built using as a donor a Yamaha 175cc motorcycle, which is normally a kick-start with a clutch-operated manual gearbox. This does mean that to start the Buggy you have to turn on the fuel tap, switch on the ignition, select a gear (probably 2nd or 3rd), depress the clutch and have a helper push you at a suitable speed. Release the clutch and the engine will start. However, in the past I've regularly started a kart single-handed by lifting the kart onto a block to raise the wheels clear of the ground,

turning the fuel tap on, switching on the ignition and turning one of the back wheels until the compression stroke is felt, and then spinning and releasing the wheel. Once you've developed the knack it becomes a speedy operation. You've probably seen film of old aeroplanes being started by a member of the ground crew swinging on the propeller – the principle is the same.

However, most of the motorcycles and mopeds in the scrap yard have electric starts, which makes the process of starting a lot easier. The down side is that there is the complication of a battery, which will require maintenance and additional electrical wiring etc. Going electric or modifying a kick start is the easiest and safest way to go.

Fig. 3.1. The original Buggy on a high-speed run. (Steve Williams)

Depending on your choice of donor motorcycle, you may chose to make a Buggy with an automatic clutch/gearbox. I would recommend this for younger Buggy drivers, as piloting then becomes a two-pedal operation, using one pedal to go and one to stop.

For ease of construction and use, we have no suspension as such, the only suspension being provided by the low-pressure tyres, which for a small-capacityBuggy are ideal. Even high-capacity circuit karts don't have suspension, but this is because they run on tarmac. For an off-road vehicle with a high-capacity engine you really need to have long-travel suspension.

Again for ease of construction, I've used a solid rear axle on the Buggy, which drives both rear wheels. Normally, as there's no rear differential, there would be a tendency for the Buggy to travel straight on when the steering wheel is turned, but by careful design of the front steering geometry I've overcome this problem. Although having only one wheel driven would make the Buggy easier to steer, having two wheels driven helps to get the Buggy out of mud when stuck.

Donor motorcycles can be found with both hydraulic and cable clutches and brakes. For simplicity and ease of installation it's best to go for a cable-operated clutch, but a suitable car clutch cable should be substituted for the one from the motorcycle, as car clutch cables tend to be heavier duty and better able to cope with the greater force applied by a large boot rather than a hand on the handle bar. As you'll see later, hydraulic brakes are easier to install than cable brakes, so don't be afraid to mix and match parts from the scrap yard to get the combination you want.

I suggest that you read through the book before you start sourcing components, as this will enable you to weigh up some of the options available, and will help to ensure that you find the most appropriate parts for your own particular Buggy.

SOURCING THE PARTS

If, like me, you often work on vehicles of various sorts, you'll

Fig. 3.2. Bike breakers can be found all over the country – look in Yellow Pages, *local classifieds, etc. This yard has a good selection of Honda, Yamaha, Suzuki, MZ, etc, bikes. Very little in this picture would cost more than £25. (Steve Williams)*

probably have all sorts of parts lying around your garage or workshop, and you may well be able to put some of these to good use in your Buggy. For instance, I chose to use the Yamaha 175cc engine and gearbox in the Buggy appearing in this book purely because it had been lying forlornly in a corner of my garage for several years!

If you don't already have the components you need to build your Buggy, the first port of call should be your local scrapyard or motorcycle dismantler. It's a sad fact that the majority of motorcycle MoT failures end up in scrapyards because they are not worth repairing. Older, small-capacity motorcycles are so cheap and plentiful second-hand that if a bike fails the MoT test due, for example, to corroded wheels, or worn or seized brakes, it's often more economic to scrap the machine and buy another cheap example than it is to buy new parts or overhaul existing ones. Consequently, it's possible to find discarded motorcycles in scrapyards or at dismantlers that have many perfectly serviceable components in spite of having failed an MoT.

At the time of writing, the majority of these yards would collect a complete motorcycle free of charge, or pay the owner a few pounds if it was delivered to them. (The scrapyard would expect to recover anything from around £50 to several hundred pounds, depending on the type of motorcycle, from the sale of the major components, the remainder being crushed for scrap value.) Bear in mind that one of the advantages of visiting a scrapyard or dismantler is that you'll be able to mix and match components from various different motorcycles, rather than relying on a single donor for everything. If you go along to your local yard and have a chat with the manager, explaining to him that you want to use the components to build a Buggy, the chances are that he'll be

sympathetic to your cause, and will let you have the parts you need for a reasonable price. However, if this fails, in order to get your donor motorcycle for the minimum possible cost, you need to purchase direct from the owner. How do you find the motorcycle you want?

First, it's worth going to the place responsible for the donor motorcycle being scrapped – the MoT garage. Tell them you're looking for a scrap bike, and explain to them what you want it for. With luck, they may already know of a suitable example that has failed the test recently, and be able to put you in touch with the owner; or they may be prepared to let you know when the next one comes along.

If this doesn't bear fruit, the second stage is to advertise in your local shop or newsagent's window. A typical advert would read:

Wanted
Honda C70
MoT failure or unroadworthy
Fair price paid
Contact: I. Wannabike
Tel. No. 01234 567890

Don't forget that the owner of this type of bike has probably been told by the scrapyard that it can be collected but no payment will be made, so your offer of a few pounds should not sound unreasonable.

It's also worth following the small advertisements in your local newspapers. Ask your friends to pass the word around at work and generally keep your eyes open.

WHAT YOU NEED FROM YOUR DONOR MOTORCYCLE

The following is a list of parts that you need to take from your donor motorcycle, and if you haven't tackled this sort of dismantling job before, it's worth buying a copy of the *Haynes Service and Repair Manual* for the relevant motorcycle. This will also be of help if you decide to overhaul any of the components, but keeping to the budget price means that there is not a lot of scope for this, and you need to ensure that, before buying the motorcycle, its engine, gearbox and any other

Fig. 3.3. This MZ motorcycle was for sale for £25. It was running, but had failed the MoT due to the exhaust. It has everything you need, including a hydraulic front brake. (Steve Williams)

components which you intend to use are in good running order.

Engine and gearbox (complete with carburettor, ignition system, exhaust system and clutch)
Chain
Sprockets
Front brake disc
Brake caliper
Hand-brake and master cylinder
Throttle cable
Various springs, clips, nuts, bolts, washers and brackets
Selection of nuts, bolts and washers to suit components removed from donor motorcycle

If you are using an engine with electric start in your Buggy, you'll need to take the associated wiring, a battery, and ideally an acid-proof battery box from the donor motorcycle.

Engine and gearbox

The Buggy described in this book uses an air-cooled, two-stroke engine (in this case a Yamaha 175cc unit). These engines are characteristically strong and reliable, although they tend to be noisier than equivalent water-cooled units and rev higher to achieve the same power. Four-stroke engines are often, but not always, water-cooled and tend to be quieter, lower revving and, at lower speeds, more user friendly which may be important for younger drivers. A major downside for a water-cooled engine is the need for a radiator and the associated plumbing. The radiator needs to be positioned in the airflow for efficient cooling and, on a vehicle that is likely to get some rough treatment, protecting it from damage could be difficult. The obvious position for the radiator would be above and behind the driver's head, but I would caution strongly against this, as in the event of damage or coolant spillage the last thing you want is boiling hot water over your head and down the back of your neck!

When looking for a suitable

engine in the scrapyard, try to find a motorcycle that hasn't been stood out in the open for too long. Perhaps have a word with the yard manager, tell him what you're looking for, and tell him what you want to use it for. Invariably he'll be helpful.

My experience has shown that you'll be unable to get the engine to run in the motorcycle frame, because the battery will be flat or missing, or there will be vital components missing, such as an HT lead. Do ensure that the engine will turn over freely, and make sure that all essential components are present, such as the carburettor, gear-change lever, exhaust, etc. If the engine is from an accident-damaged bike, check thoroughly to make sure that there is no impact damage, and pay particular attention to the crankcase and various alloy covers. Try selecting all the gears – if you move the drive sprocket back and forth whilst doing this, it will help the gears to engage with a healthy click. Frequently there's superficial damage to the engine if the motorcycle has been dropped, but ensure that the covers are not distorted, which may give you oil leak problems.

Beware of any engine with a spark plug missing, as if water has entered, it will almost certainly have caused damage such as seized piston rings, and the gearbox components will be sitting in water, not oil, which will cause the gears to seize.

If possible, and if you're familiar with working on motorcycle engines, remove the cylinder head and check the condition of the piston and bearings.

Chain and sprockets

It's a good idea to check the condition of the chain and sprockets before removing the components from the motorcycle. To check the chain, shift the bike gearbox into neutral, then check the entire length of the chain for damaged rollers, loose links and pins and, on sealed chains, missing O-rings. If lubrication has been neglected, corrosion may have caused the chain links to bind and kink. If this is the case, any such links should be thoroughly cleaned and worked free.

The condition of the sprockets should also be checked – you'll probably need to remove the sprocket cover from the gearbox to check the drive sprocket. Check the sprocket teeth for wear and damage.

If any of the chain or sprocket components are excessively worn, and you're unable to find alternative second-hand components in good condition, you may have to resort to buying new components. Note that if you mix old and new components, you're likely to find that the new component(s) wear more rapidly than usual. It's good practice not to fit a new chain to old sprockets, and not

Alternative solutions

Automatic clutch

The Honda 70 is a strong, reliable, four-stroke, air-cooled engine with an automatic clutch and three gears. This engine will not run away with a youngster, and can be operated with just two foot controls – the accelerator and the brake. Additionally, both pedals can be operated with the right foot (as on a car), reducing the chance of the driver getting confused and operating both at the same time. This also provides the option of fitting a larger engine with a clutch at a later date – the clutch pedal could then be fitted in the conventional place and the driver would already be used to the accelerator and brake being in the correct place.

Fig. 3.4. The main items used from the donor motorcycle are the engine, gearbox, brake caliper, disc, sprocket and chain. (Steve Williams)

use the old chain if you fit new sprockets – renew the chain and sprockets as a set.

Brake components

Before removing the brake components from the motorcycle, check their condition as follows. Check that the disc is not pitted with rust, or scored. Try the caliper operation by squeezing the brake lever and moving the motorcycle forward. If the brake is in working order, it should not be possible .to move the motorcycle. Equally importantly, when the handgrip is released, do the brake pads release from the disc? If they do, we're off to a good start. It may be worth dismantling the caliper and master

Fig. 3.5. A disc and caliper both in good order. The disc looks fairly new and you can see from the bright shiny surface finish that the bike was in use until recently. Beware of buying a donor bike that has been laid up for a while and has a rusty disc and, possibly, a seized caliper. (Steve Williams)

cylinder with the aid of the relevant motorcycle workshop manual. Certainly renew the pads, and possibly renew the caliper piston seals and master cylinder seals. Please note that brake fluid is an effective paint stripper and melter

of plastic, including some trainer soles. Take care not to get fluid in your eyes – if you do, flush out with plenty of water, and seek medical attention. I suffer from dermatitis caused by many years of exposure to brake fluid.

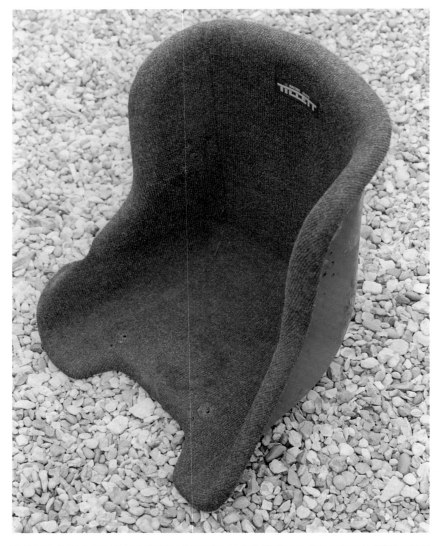

Fig. 3.6. This is a second-hand go-kart seat which cost £15, but the moulded seat from a stacking chair could be used and will only cost £1 to £2, if anything. (Steve Williams)

PARTS YOU REQUIRE FROM ELSEWHERE

Other parts required, additional to those taken from the donor motorcycle, are as follows. This list does not include the metal stock materials required, which are listed separately later in this Chapter.

Suffolk Colt lawnmower fuel tank, complete with on/off tap, fuel pipe and vented screw cap.
Two hose clips to suit fuel pipe
Four or six Ford differential flanges
Four quad-bike wheels and tyres
Steering wheel
Seat
2 self-centring bearings for rear axle
Conduit saddle clamp block for 19mm (3/4in) diameter conduit (for mounting steering column)
4 off track-rod ends (can be fabricated – see text)
8 off nuts to fit track-rod ends
3 bolts to fit through track-rod ends (with self-locking nuts)
1 bolt for steering column (with self-locking nut)
2 off M16 x 160mm long bolts for steering pivots (with self-locking nuts)* (see note on following page)
2m of 3/16in copper brake pipe and suitable fittings
4 off washers 3mm thick with 25mm diameter holes
4 off phosphor-bronze washers with 25mm diameter holes

Fig. 3.7. Two of these proprietary self-centring bearings will be required. The internal diameter should match the diameter of the selected rear axle shaft. Look under bearing factors in Yellow Pages. (Steve Williams)

2 off split-pins 3mm diameter x 40mm long
Assorted tension springs (to use as pedal return springs)
Clutch cable from car – see Chapter 8.
Accelerator cable from car – see Chapter 8.
Selection of split- pins
Assorted bolts, washers and Nyloc nuts
Cable ties
Paint and primer
Chain oil
Quantity of 2in nails for holding frame tube on board whilst welding
8ft x 4ft x 18mm board for marking out frame

*Note that the nuts and bolts obtained for use as stub-axle pivots must match the thick wall tube used for tubes U and V. Each bolt must be a good, but not tight fit, in the tube.

Fuel tank

The Suffolk Colt lawnmower fuel tank has a capacity of about one litre which will provide for about one hour of use. A lawnmower tank was selected because not only did it have a screw cap and an on/off tap which could be positioned so that the driver could reach it but because of the small diameter of the fuel pipe. While providing sufficient fuel for the engine the flow rate from the pipe would be low in the event of the pipe getting damaged. These types of fuel tank are readily available, even new, from lawnmower shops.

Ford differential flanges

The differential flanges used on the original Buggy were obtained from rear wheel drive Fords such as the Mk2 Escort, Cortina, Capri or Sierra.

The Buggy appearing in this book uses four flanges, one for each of the back wheels, one for the brake disc and one for the drive sprocket. If you're planning to use large wheels (fixed by studs or

Fig. 3.8. A fuel tank from a lawnmower. Note the ventilated screw cap and on/off fuel tap, both desirable safety features. (Steve Williams)

bolts) on the front of the Buggy, then a further two flanges may be required, one for each front wheel.

Wheels and tyres

The original Buggy uses four quad-bike wheels and tyres, which were bought new from a farm machinery factors. These wheels and tyres are not cheap, but are perfectly suited for use on an off-road Buggy.

To keep costs down it would be worth keeping an eye open for some second-hand wheels and tyres or, alternatively, wheels from a small car such as a Mini could be used. Bear in mind that if

Fig. 3.9. A Ford differential flange, in this case from a Ford Capri, obtained for £2.50 from a scrapyard. (Steve Williams)

conventional wheels and tyres are used, the Buggy's off-road ability will be somewhat compromised. It's also important to note that the diameter of the wheels determines the Buggy's ground clearance, so if very small diameter wheels are used, the ground clearance will be limited. A 6inch (150mm) ground clearance is the sensible minimum required. Also note that it's highly advisable to incorporate wheel bearings into the design – the wheels on the original Buggy run on needle roller bearings which are incorporated in tubes welded to each wheel.

THE STOCK METAL MATERIALS YOU WILL NEED (FACTORY OFFCUTS/SALE STOCK/NEW)

18m of 38mm (1½in) diameter round mild steel tube, with minimum 16swg (1.6mm) wall thickness – for Buggy frame
600mm x 600mm (24in x 26in) sheet of 1.6mm (16swg) thick steel plate – for Buggy floor
600mm x 600mm (24in x 24in) sheet of 5mm thick steel plate – for brackets and plates
400mm length of 30mm x 10mm flat steel bar (strip) – for front stub-axle carriers
320mm length of 25mm diameter round steel bar (or bar of a diameter to suit the front wheels/bearings you intend to use) – for front stub axles
800mm length of 19mm diameter, 1.6mm (3/4in) wall thickness steel tube – for steering column
1000mm length of 30mm diameter solid steel bar – for rear axle* (see note on following page)
140mm length of 22mm diameter steel tube, 3mm minimum wall thickness – for steering pivot housings, tubes U and V (see text)
1000mm length of 13mm diameter steel tube, with internal diameter

Fig. 3.10. These balloon tyres were sourced from a farm machinery factors and are usually used on quad bikes. The hubs have the same stud pattern as Mini wheels and come complete with bearings. (Steve Williams)

Ducks and dives

Seat

The original Buggy uses a bucket seat, but any alternative that fits within the Buggy frame can be used, provided it is comfortable for the intended driver.

A plastic stacking chair can be adapted to provide more support for the driver by fitting aluminium sides to it and securing with nuts and bolts or rivets to give it more rigidity and to make it more like a bucket seat.

greater than the thread diameter of the thread diameter of the track-rod ends you intend to use – for track rods
Length of steel tube to fit from gear-change splined shaft on gearbox to outer frame tube – see Chapter 8.
2000mm length of 20mm x 5mm flat steel bar – for pedals
*The rear axle is made from 30mm solid bar steel stock. When buying material to make the axle, take advice from the stockholder – hard steel must be used, not malleable steel, as if the axle is malleable, it may bend after rigorous off-road use.

Proprietary axles can be bought from karting specialists, in which case bearings and wheel mounting flanges can be bought to suit, although this is likely to be a more expensive option than making your own axle. Kart axles are designed to withstand the rigours of karting, so should be perfectly adequate for the Buggy.

Sourcing the steel materials

I found that I needed a work plan to ensure I made, sourced and purchased parts in some fairly logical order and, as the basis of the Buggy is the frame, onto which are bolted all the other components, it was decided to give early priority to sourcing the steel tube.

The Buggy's frame is a space-frame construction with round-section tubes, which makes an incredibly light and strong structure, resistant to loads both in compression and tension. The frame is made from a number of lengths of tube, but due to the lengths of some of the tubes, the longest being just over 2.6m, it's unlikely that you'll be able to source all the material required from offcuts. It should be possible to cut all the frame tubes required from three standard 6.1m lengths of tube, which can be bought from a steel stockholder.

When you go to buy the tubing

for your frame, explain to the stockholder that you're going to use it to build a Buggy – this will help to ensure that you end up with the most suitable material for the job, and you may well find that if the stockholder is sympathetic to your cause he'll be able to find a few offcuts which will help to reduce the cost of the project. It would be a good idea to take along a list of all the metal materials needed to build your Buggy, as you're likely to be able to negotiate a good deal to buy all the materials from one supplier.

The wall thickness of the frame tubing should be at least 16swg. The 'swg' stands for 'standard wire gauge', a traditional standard for measuring not only the thickness of wire but also sheet steel and, in our case, the wall thickness of our tube. To help you identify it, 16swg is about 1/16in (1.6mm). The higher the number, the thinner the wall thickness, eg, 18swg is thinner than 16swg. 16swg (1.6mm) is the minimum wall thickness for the frame tubing. If the only material available is of thicker section or slightly larger diameter it will be quite suitable. Also, don't disregard SHS (square hollow section) or RHS (rectangular hollow section) tubing which are both quite suitable for the job.

Some people might prefer the easier to cut mitre joints and angles you get when using RHS or SHS, instead of having to 'fish-mouth' the round tube. However in my opinion a frame constructed from round tube does look more pleasing and less agricultural.

I'm fortunate in that I live close to a town with a steel making and engineering tradition, and there are at least a dozen engineering companies and steel fabricators, all a source of offcuts. A search through your *Yellow Pages* will enable you to find such companies local to you. I advise a very polite and careful approach when requesting offcuts, and if you're refused it may be that they are mindful of safety and insurance regulations and don't allow visitors to rummage through scrap bins or skips. But, with a bit of luck you should be able to purchase all your steel quite reasonably.

A point worth mentioning is that if your tube is sourced from several different places, ensure that it's all to the same specification.

If you don't see yourself singing 'any old iron' round the metal merchants, you could purchase new standard lengths from your local steel stockholder, indeed it's advisable to do so for the main frame tubing.

Fig. 3.11. Samples of steel tube. If you get offered a good deal on square tube, don't be frightened to make the whole frame from square, although most feel that round tube looks better and gives a 'tougher' image. Whatever you do, do not go for material with a wall thickness of less than 1.6mm (16swg). We used material with a 3mm wall thickness. (Steve Williams)

Chapter 4

Making the frame

The Buggy frame is constructed entirely from 38mm (1½in) seamed round mild steel tube, with a minimum 16swg (1.6mm) wall thickness. You'll need about 18m of tubing. If you're purchasing new material from a steel stockholder, it's likely to be supplied in 6.1m lengths, and you'll therefore need 3 lengths to give the 18m you require. However, remember that you have to be careful with the way you cut the material up, because when you end up with two lengths 1m long, and you realise that you need a 1.4m long piece you can feel a bit silly! This is particularly important if the supplier is cutting the material up for you into 2 or 3m lengths so you can get it home in your car or on a trailer.

The strength and integrity of the frame will only be as good as the accuracy of your construction and the quality of your welding, so, this is the most important part of building your Buggy. Take great care with your measurements, and never feel ashamed at asking a qualified engineer and/or welder to check your work.

Fig. 4.1. The finished Buggy frame in all its glory! (Steve Williams)

WHAT YOU NEED

Tools required

Welding set
Welding mask or goggles, gloves,
overalls and safety boots
Steel tape measure
Steel ruler and set square
Hacksaw
Files – one flat, one round
Wire brush
Tank/hole saw or jigsaw
Electric drill with a selection of
drill bits

Materials required

For the frame you will need:
18m of 38mm (1½in) diameter
round mild steel tube, with
minimum 16swg (1.6mm) wall
thickness – for Buggy frame
600mm x 600mm (24in x 26in)
sheet of 1.6mm (16swg) thick steel
plate – for Buggy floor
600mm x 600mm (24in x 24in)
sheet of 5mm thick steel plate –
for brackets and plates
Quantity of 2in nails for holding
frame tube on board whilst
welding
8ft x 4ft x 18mm board for
marking out frame

CUTTING FRAME TUBES TO LENGTH

Please note that the dimensions given for the Buggy I built are intended to give a frame big enough for youths and adults, approximately 15 years old and upward. The actual dimensions of the tubes are not critical – variations are quite acceptable. Also, for the Buggy I built, I tapered the frame towards the front (ie, tubes A and B are closer together at the front of the vehicle than at the rear) for purely cosmetic reasons. The dimensions given in this Chapter for the tube lengths will enable you to construct a Buggy with a square frame (ie, tubes A and B are parallel), which is easier to build.

I would recommend that you don't cut all the tubes before you start constructing your frame, but instead cut tubes in pairs, tack-weld them in position and then measure the frame to find the required length for the next pair. Remember, measure twice cut once. It's a good idea to identify each length of tubing by marking it with a felt-tip pen. Take care when

cutting to ensure that the tube ends are cut square, with the exception of one end of each of the tubes I, J, L and M, which need to be cut at an angle to ensure a correct fit with tube K. Tubes I and J need one end to be cut at an angle of 25° and tubes L and M need to be cut at an angle of 34°.

For details of the tubes required, refer to Fig. 4.2, and to the following cutting lists. The second list suggests how best to cut the lengths required from three standard 6.1m lengths of tube, which can be bought from a steel stockholder.

The following lengths need to be cut from the 38mm (1½ in) diameter, 16swg steel tube:

Tube	Length
A and B	1651mm
C	1016mm
D	760mm
E, F, G and H	600mm
I and J	1410mm
K	2650mm
L and M	1110mm
N, O and P	285mm
Q and R	630mm
S and T	360mm

Fig. 4.2. The complete Buggy frame showing tube identification letters.

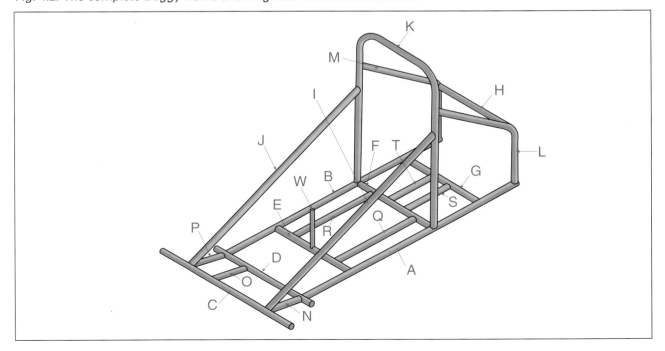

Sample cutting list based on three 6.1m lengths of material:

Length No1		Length No2		Length No3	
Tube	Cut length	Tube	Cut length	Tube	Cut length
A	1651mm	C	1016mm	D	760mm
B	1651mm	E	600mm	J	1410mm
K	2650mm	F	600mm	L	1110mm
		G	600mm	M	1110mm
		H	600mm	P	285mm
		I	1410mm	R	630mm
		N	285mm	S	360mm
		O	285mm	T	360mm
		Q	630mm		

FISH-MOUTHING

To get a good fit when mating the round-section frame tubes together, with the exception of both ends of tube C and one end of tubes A, B and W, all the ends of the tubes must be 'fish-mouthed'.

This can be achieved either by hand, using a half or full-round file, or if you have access to a proper fish-mouthing machine then this makes the whole job easier. It may be worth visiting a local fabrication or engineering shop to see if they can do the job for you – look in your local *Yellow Pages*.

Fig. 4.3. A finished fish-mouthed tube. (Steve Williams)

Fig. 4.4. Most people won't have one of these, but a proper fish-mouthing machine will make the job quicker an easier. (Steve Williams)

Ducks and dives

The toilet roll trick

To produce the fish-mouths on the ends of the tubes I've used the toilet roll trick. Refer to Appendix 1 for templates which can be used to fish-mouth tubes using 'The toilet roll trick'.

Using thin card, roll a tube of the same diameter as the steel tube to be shaped. To ensure the diameter is correct, the card can be rolled around the steel tube, and secured with sticky tape or elastic bands. Make sure that the card tube retains its shape when sliding it from the steel tube.

Hold the end of the card tube against the steel tube to be joined to, and mark on the card the approximate shape of the steel tube. (Steve Williams)

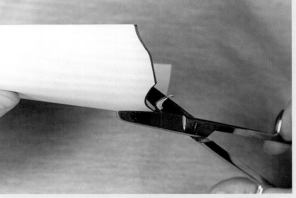

Trim the card tube with scissors to get a good fit. Ideally the fish-mouth should cover half the tube it is to fit. (Steve Williams)

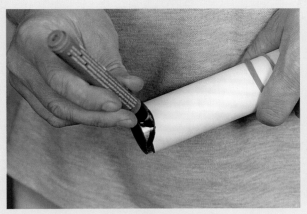

Slide the cardboard tube over the steel tube to be shaped and mark the fish-mouth outline on the steel tube with a felt-tip marker pen. (Steve Williams)

File the tube to shape using a half-round file. (Steve Williams)

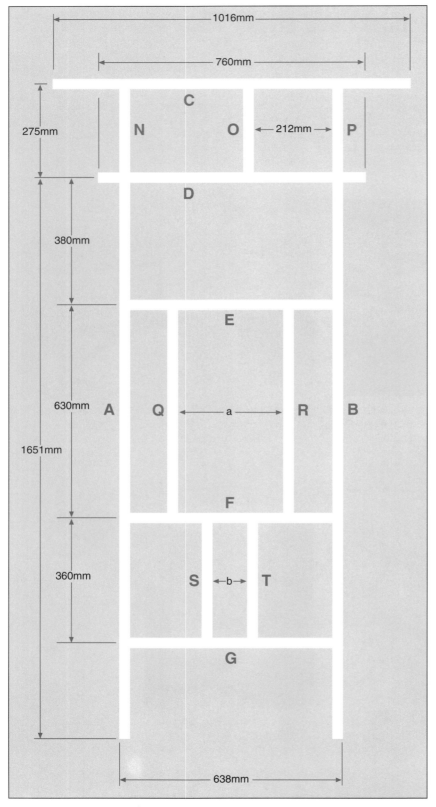

Fig. 4.5. Dimensions for marking out the frame building board showing the positions of the main frame tubes.

FRAME BUILDING BOARD

The building board provides a good flat surface on which to construct your Buggy frame. You may find it useful to mark out the positions of the frame tubes on the building board before you start. The distance between tubes Q and R (dimension a) is governed by the width between the fixing points of your chosen seat, while the distance between tubes S and T (dimension b) depends on the dimensions of the engine and gearbox you have acquired for your Buggy.

Fig. 4.6. The frame building board used for the original Buggy. Note that the frame tapers towards the front for purely cosmetic reasons. (Steve Williams)

Ducks and dives

The angle trick

Use the corner of a square piece of paper or card to give you a 90° angle. Folding the paper diagonally in half will give you a 45° angle. Don't worry if this sounds crude – as a professional engineer I still reach for a piece of paper when I want a right-angle.

FRAME CONSTRUCTION

After cutting and fish-mouthing frame tubes A and B at one end, place them on the building board (fish-mouth end towards tube D) and hold them in position by knocking 2in nails into the board. Each tube can be held using four nails, two at either side of each tube at each end.

Next, prepare tube D by first cutting to length. Both ends of tube D require fish-mouthing, but to fit the diameter of tubes U and V (which house the steering pivot pins) and at an angle of 10° so that when tubes U and V fitted they are inclined towards each other, ie towards the centre of the frame, at the top (see Chapter 5, Fig. 5.5).

Place tube D in position on the board ensuring that the ends of tube D stick out equal amounts from tubes A and B. Also make sure that the fish-mouths of tube D are correctly orientated so that when tubes U and V are in position they will lean in towards the centre of the frame at the top. Additionally, the fish-mouths of tube D must be orientated so that when tubes U and V are in position they will lean towards the rear of the Buggy at the top, at an angle of 15° (again, see Chapter 5, Fig. 5.6).

Hold tube D in position with 2in nails, ensuring that the angles mentioned previously are correct, and tack-weld to tubes A and B.

Cut and fish-mouth tubes E, F and G, place them in position on the building board, hold with nails and tack-weld to tubes A and B.

You'll now have to remove the assembly from the building board while you make the front kick-up sub-assembly. Even with only the tack-welds in place the assembly should be strong enough to move.

The front of the Buggy has a 50mm (2in) kick-up. Cut and fish-mouth tubes N, O and P, and cut tube C – remember that C is one of the few tubes which does not require fish-mouthing. This kick-up sub-assembly is first made as a flat assembly before being tack-welded to tube D to give the 50mm kick-up. Place tube C on the building board and hold in position with nails. Offer up tubes N, O and P and secure in the correct positions with nails, making sure that tube C sticks out equally beyond tubes N and P, and that the distance between tubes N and P is the same as that between tubes A and B on the main frame assembly. Note that tube O is not in the middle of the frame, but is offset to the right-hand side. Tack-weld tubes N, O and P to tube C. Also note that the dimensions for the frame layout shown in Fig. 4.5 take account of the 50mm kick-up, so when laid flat tubes O, N and P will appear longer than they are actually drawn on the building board.

Remove the front kick-up sub-assembly from the board, then manoeuvre the main frame assembly back into position and

Fig. 4.7. Method for ensuring the correct angle for the kick-up at the front of the Buggy frame.

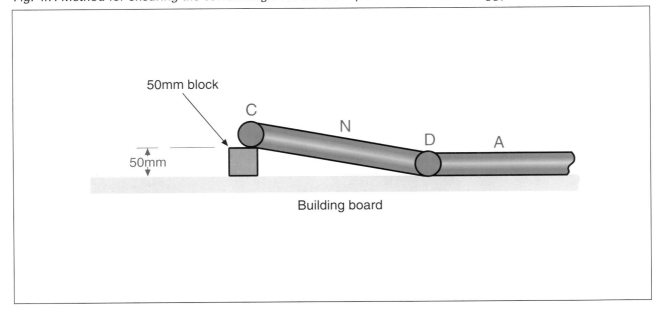

50mm block

50mm

C

N

D

A

Building board

hold with the nails. Place the kick-up sub-assembly in position against the main frame, supporting tube C on a 50mm high block to give the required kick-up. Position the sub-assembly so that tubes N, O, and P are correctly located on tube D of the main frame, then tack-weld into position.

The next tubes to be added to the frame are tubes Q, R, S and T. Tubes Q and R provide the support for the seat, while tubes S and T provide the support for the engine/gearbox mountings. I would suggest that you measure your frame from the centre line of tube E to the centre line of tube F at the required positions of tubes Q and R to make sure that the recommended cut lengths are still going to be correct. This check should also be carried out between tubes F and G to ensure that the cut length of tubes S and T are going to be correct.

When you're sure that you have the correct lengths for the tubes, cut and fish-mouth tubes Q and R,

then position them on the board, hold the tubes with nails and tack-weld in position. Remember that the seat you are using governs the distance between the two tubes.

Now repeat the procedure with tubes S and T, but this time it's the engine/gearbox you have chosen and the distance between its mountings that will dictate the spacing required between the two tubes.

You now have the basic frame and it's time to fit the roll bar and the rest of the structure. The roll bar, tube K, can be made in one of three ways depending on the equipment available to you.

The photographs in this book show a Buggy with a roll bar which was produced using a tube bender. It's unlikely that the average home builder is going to have the necessary equipment to bend 38mm diameter tube, however it may be possible to hire or borrow a heavy duty pipe bender or to have the roll bar produced by a local fabrication shop.

Alternative methods of producing the roll bar are shown in Figs. 4.8, 4.9 and 4.10. Fig. 4.10 shows a roll bar which has had 'V's cut out to allow the tube to be bent, after which it has been re-welded. A simpler method is to cut and mitre the tube and make the roll bar out of five pieces as shown in Figs. 4.8 and 4.9. Having made the roll bar using your chosen method, it can be tack-welded into position on tubes A and B, ensuring that the roll bar (tube K) is positioned parallel to tube F on the main frame.

Mark onto the roll bar (tube K) the height/position where the side tubes I and J will join it, and measure the distance from the roll bar to tube C to ensure that the recommended cut length for tubes I and J is still correct. Cut and fish-mouth tubes I and J, remembering that one end of each should be cut at an angle of 25°. Position the square-cut end of tube I on tube C outboard of tube A, and position the angled end of tube I against the

Fig. 4.8. The dimensions for the roll bar. The roll bar can be formed either by bending or fabricating.

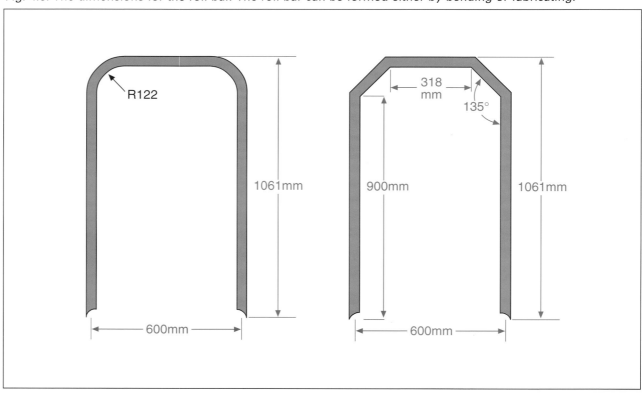

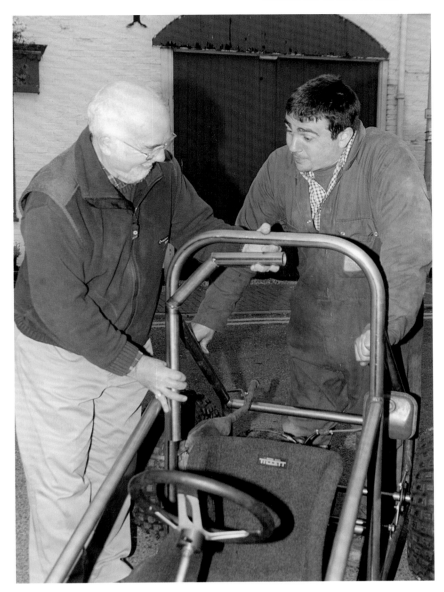

Left: Fig. 4.9. An alternative method for producing the roll bar if you don't have access to a tube bender is to fabricate from sections of tube cut at an angle. (Steve Williams)

Above: Fig. 4.10. It's possible to produce a curved roll bar by cutting a series of 'V's out of the tube, bending it round and re-welding. (Steve Williams)

roll bar (tube K). Tack-weld tube I in position, and then repeat the procedure on the other side of the frame with tube J.

Tubes L and M require cutting, fish-mouthing and then bending or mitring in a similar fashion to the roll bar (tube K) – see Fig. 4.12. Note that one end of each of the tubes should be cut and fish-mouthed at an angle of 34° to allow it to mate to the roll bar (tube K). Once made, tubes L and M can be positioned on tubes A and B and

Left: Fig. 4.11. Main frame tube I tacked in position. Note the excellent fit produced by fish-mouthing the tubes. (Steve Williams)

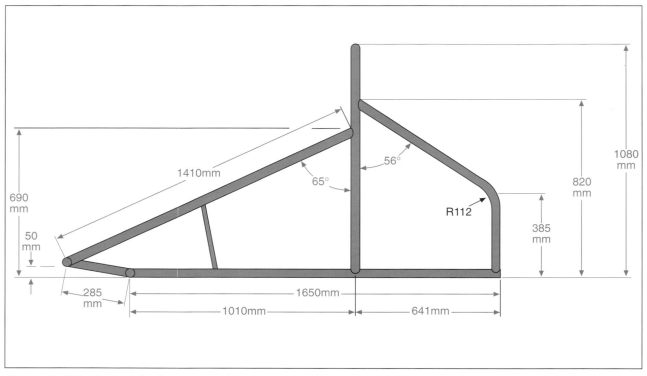

Fig. 4.12. Side view of the frame showing the dimensions and positions of the main frame tubes.

Fig. 4.13. The bearing mounting plate needs to be made to suit the bearings you have purchased. The 30mm wide slot is to allow the rear axle assembly to be removed without having to remove the sprocket, wheel hubs, bearings, etc. It, therefore, needs to be slightly wider than the diameter of your axle.

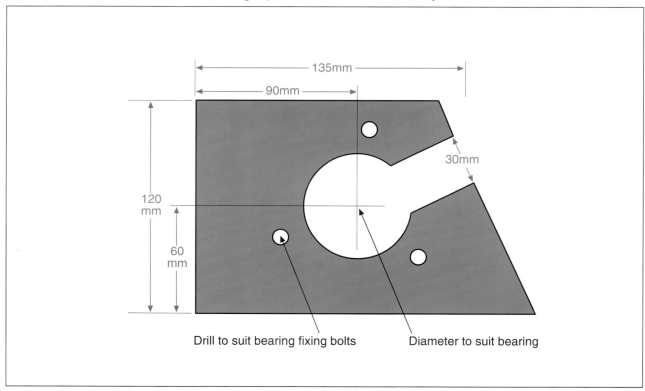

Ducks and dives

The string trick

In awkward places, or when you want to measure round corners or funny shapes, I find that a piece of string can be useful tool. Use a piece of string to find the distance you want, and then it's easy to measure the length of the string once it's straightened out with your tape measure.

mated up with the roll bar before being tack-welded in place.

The last frame tube to be fitted is tube H, which fits at the rear of the frame between tubes L and M. Tube H should be positioned in the centre of the bend in tubes L and M. Measure the distance between tubes L and M to check that the recommended length for tube H is correct before cutting. Once the tube has been cut and fish-mouthed, tack-weld it in position.

The bare frame is now complete, and all the components have been

tack-welded in position, however before final welding, the various mounting plates and brackets should be made and fitted to the frame as follows.

REAR AXLE BEARING MOUNTING PLATES

From your piece of 5mm steel plate mark out and cut the two rear-axle bearing mounting plates – see Fig. 4.13. The outside profile of the plates can be quite easily cut using

a hacksaw or an electric jig saw. The holes for the bearings can be cut using a tank/hole saw or, again, can be cut out with a jigsaw. The bearing holes and fixing bolt holes should be cut to suit the bearings you've purchased.

Once the correct position of the mounting plates has been determined, they can be tack-welded in position on the left-hand side of the frame where tube A joins tube L, and on the right-hand side of the frame where tube B joins tube M.

ENGINE/GEARBOX MOUNTING PLATES

Cut the engine/gearbox mounting plates from 5mm plate. These you'll have to make to suit your chosen engine/gearbox – Fig. 4.15 shows the ones I used for my Yamaha 175cc unit.

To determine the size and shape of the mounting plates, stand the engine/gearbox in the back of the chassis in the approximately required position. Before attempting anything else, satisfy yourself that you have access to the kick-start mechanism, if required, and that the engine is in the original attitude that it was mounted in the bike frame – this is essential for the correct working of the carburettor float chamber and the engine lubrication system (the dipstick and oil filler plug are only accurate with the engine mounted in its original attitude). Once the engine/gearbox is located correctly in the frame, look at the existing lugs on the crankcase and make up brackets to mount the engine in the Buggy. If desired, additional frame tubes can be added to aid engine/gearbox mounting. Note that the mounting brackets should be of at least equal thickness to the original brackets used to mount the unit in the bike. To make the process easier, use wooden dummy brackets or stiff card templates, mark the shape of the bracket(s) and the positions of the mounting bolt holes, and then transfer the marks to the metal plate.

Fig. 4.14. The bearing plates are positioned on the left-hand side of the frame where tube A joins tube L, and on the right-hand side where tube B joins tube M.

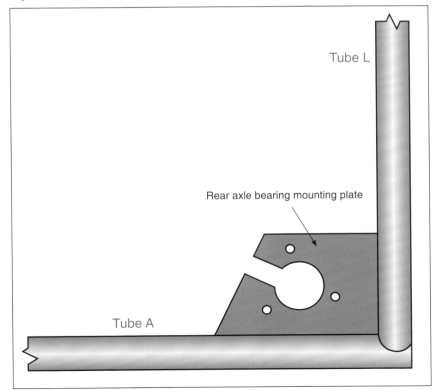

Tube L

Rear axle bearing mounting plate

Tube A

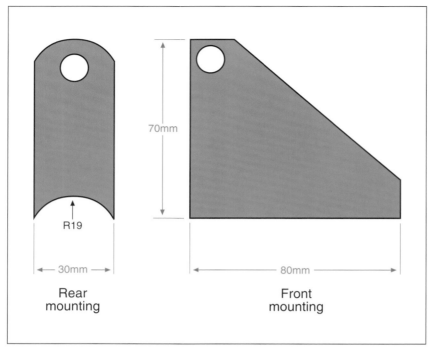

Fig. 4.15. You will have to make mounts to suit the engine/gearbox from your donor motorcycle. These are the ones I made for my Yamaha 175cc unit.

engine/gearbox, but it would be a good idea to wait until the plates have been welded to the frame and the rear axle has been trial fitted – this will enable you to drill the holes in the right place.

On some engines, such as the Honda 50 and 70, it may be possible to produce an engine mounting plate with slotted holes to allow adjustment of the chain tension. Alternatively, to allow chain tension adjustment, use elongated holes for the rear axle mounting (but note that these cannot be used with self-centring bearings).

When you're sure that you have the correct mounting plate positions for your particular engine/gearbox, the plates can be tack-welded in place. For the engine/gearbox I used, the front plates were tack-welded to tubes S and T, and the rear plates were tack-welded in place on tube G. You may, of course, need to vary this arrangement, according on the mountings fitted to your chosen engine/gearbox.

Once you've decided on the size, shape and position of the mounting plates, they can be cut out using a hacksaw or an electric jigsaw. At this stage you can drill the mounting holes for the

Fig. 4.16. One of the two front engine/gearbox mounting plates. This one is shown fully welded. (Steve Williams)

Fig. 4.17. The rear engine/gearbox mounting plates. Again, fully welded. (Steve Williams)

Alternative solutions

Adjustable engine/gearbox mountings

To enable adjustment of the chain tension, the engine/ gearbox mountings can be designed to allow the engine/ gearbox position to be altered slightly. For the Honda 70 engine, this can be achieved using two flat plates, one bolted to the engine, and one welded to the frame. The arrangement shown here was loosely copied from a racing kart. The plates should be wide enough to fit between frame tubes S and T. Drill the top plate to accept four bolts, which will be used to bolt the top plate to the bottom plate. With the top plate drilled, clamp the two plates together, mark the locations of the holes in the top plate on the bottom plate, then drill corresponding holes in the bottom plate. Cut the heads off the four bolts, then weld the bolts in position in the holes in the top plate, so that the ends of the bolts are flush with the top face of the plate. Elongate the holes in the bottom plate to allow the top plate to slide backwards and forwards for adjustment. Weld suitable brackets to the top plate to allow it to support the engine/ transmission (on the top plate shown here an additional plate was welded to the top plate to help support the engine/ transmission). Weld the bottom plate in position on the chassis between tubes S and T, and bolt the top plate to the engine/ transmission. The engine/ transmission can now be fitted by lowering into place, making sure that the bolts welded to the top plate pass though the elongated holes in the bottom plate. Fit Nyloc nuts to the ends of the bolts, then adjust the position of the engine/ transmission as necessary and tighten the nuts.

Bottom mounting plate welded to frame. (Derek Manders)

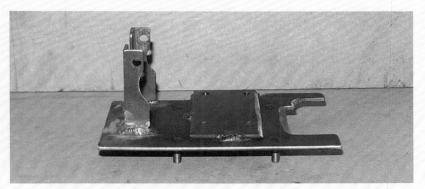

Completed top mounting plate with brackets welded in position. The holes in the brackets align with the original footrest mounting points on the engine. (Derek Manders)

Top mounting plate in position on engine/transmission. (Derek Manders)

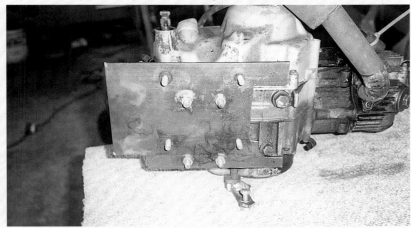

Fig. 4.18. Seat mounting plates welded in position. These have only 4 holes drilled for a non-adjustable seat. If you want the position of the seat to be adjustable, then you can drill a series of holes. (Steve Williams)

SEAT MOUNTING PLATES

Again from the 5mm plate, cut two seat mounting plates approximately 45mm x 400mm to suit the seat that you have. At this stage you can drill the fixing holes for the seat, but it would be a good idea to wait until the plates have been welded to the frame and the pedals and steering wheel have been fitted – this will enable you to drill the holes in the right place. If more than one person is likely to use the Buggy, or if you want to allow for someone who is still growing, you can drill a series of holes to allow the seat to be moved forwards or backwards.

Once you're happy with the size and positions of the mounting plates, tack-weld them in place on tubes Q and R.

FINAL WELDING OF FRAME AND MOUNTING PLATES

It's suggested at this stage that, if not already done, the axle and the engine are trial fitted to check that the mounting plates are in the right place. When you're happy with the position of all the mounting plates, the frame can be fully welded. To help prevent distortion, weld alternate sides – for example weld joint C/I followed by joint C/J, then weld joint K/I followed by K/J, etc.

FLOOR

When your frame has been fully welded, cut the floor panel from the 1.6mm steel plate. This can be made in either one or two pieces. If making it as one piece then you can either pre-form it to give the 10° kick-up at the front, or weld the kick-up in position on tubes C, D, N, O and P before clamping the remainder of the plate in position on tubes A, B and E and welding. If making the floor in two pieces, one piece can be used to panel in under tubes C, D, N, O and P, and the other to panel in between tubes A, B, D and E.

Fig. 4.19. Starting to fully weld the frame. Remember to weld alternate sides to minimise distortion. Spot the deliberate mistake – the welder should be wearing thick gloves! (Steve Williams)

Fig. 4.20. Fully welded frame tube joints. (Steve Williams)

Alternative solutions

A view of the underside of the Buggy, showing the floor mounting lugs welded to the lower frame tubes. (Derek Manders)

Full-length floor

The floor could be made full-length, but if you decide to do this on a Buggy with an air-cooled engine, be careful not to shroud the engine too much, as air-cooled engines need good airflow.

Aluminium floor

Although steel sheet is the best material to use for the floor, aluminium could be used. However, bear in mind that aluminium provides poor protection against flying stones, as it is easily punctured and damaged.

Detachable floor

If the floor is detachable, it is easier to clean the Buggy frame, and any dirt trapped between the edges of the frame and the floor can be removed. One easy method of making the floor detachable is to weld a series of lugs to the bottom of the frame lower tubes. The lugs can be tapped (with, for instance, a 6mm thread) to allow the floor fixing bolts to screw into them.

One of the screws securing the floor to the mounting lugs on the frame. (Steve Williams)

Chapter 5

Front axle and steering

When designing the Buggy, I tried to keep the front axle and steering components as simple as possible, whilst still being robust enough to stand up to off-road use. If you decide to modify any of the components from the designs shown here, make absolutely sure that they will be able to cope with the loads that are likely to be passing though them – the last thing you need when using your Buggy is to suddenly find that you have no steering! If in doubt, ask a qualified engineer and/or welder to check your work.

WHAT YOU NEED

Tools required

Welding set
Welding mask or goggles, gloves, overalls and safety boots
Steel tape measure
Steel ruler and set square
Hacksaw
Files – one flat, one round
Wire brush
Electric drill with a selection of drill bits
Socket set
Set of ring spanners
Set of open-ended spanners
Set of Allen keys
Hammer and centre punch

Materials required

400mm length of 30mm x 10mm flat steel bar (strip) – for front stub-axle carriers
320mm length of 25mm diameter round steel bar (or bar of a diameter to suit the front wheels/bearings you intend to use) – for front stub axles

800mm length of 19mm diameter, 1.6mm (3/4in) wall thickness steel tube – for steering
140mm length of 22mm diameter steel tube, 3mm minimum wall thickness – for steering pivot housings, tubes U and V (see text)*
1000mm length of 13mm diameter steel tube, with internal diameter greater than the thread diameter of the track-rod ends you intend to use – for track rods
5mm steel plate (can be cut from remainder of sheet used during frame construction) – for steering arms and various brackets and plates
4 off steel washers 3mm thick with 25mm diameter holes
4 off phosphor-bronze washers with 25mm diameter holes

2 off split-pins 3mm diameter x 40mm long
2 off M16 x 160mm long bolts for steering pivots (with self-locking nuts)*
Conduit saddle clamp block for 19mm (3/4in) diameter conduit (for mounting steering column)
4 off track-rod ends (can be fabricated – see text)
8 off nuts to fit track-rod ends
3 bolts to fit through track-rod ends (with self-locking nuts)
1 bolt for steering column (with self-locking nut)
*Note that the nuts and bolts obtained for use as stub-axle pivots must match the thick wall tube used for tubes U and V. Each bolt must be a good, but not tight fit, in the tube.

Fig. 5.1. The parts required to make the stub-axle carrier. You need four of the smaller pieces and two of the larger ones to complete the two carriers.

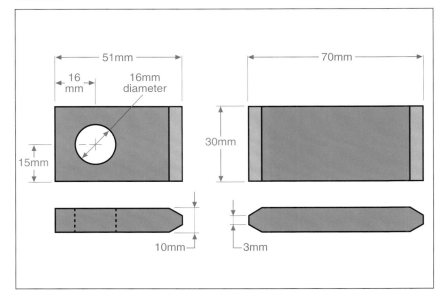

Fig. 5.2. The parts required to make the stub-axle carrier and a set of parts already tack-welded together. (Steve Williams)

MAKING THE STUB-AXLE CARRIERS

From the 30mm x 10mm flat steel bar cut two sets of the three pieces required to make the stub-axle carrier – see Fig. 5.1. The bar can be cut using a hacksaw or an electric jigsaw.

Using a centre punch, mark the position of the 16mm diameter hole (or a size appropriate for the steering pivot bolts you intend to use) on each of the four smaller pieces of metal. Working on each piece in turn, ensure that the metal is securely clamped, and then drill the hole.

In preparation for welding, working on each of the components in turn, file or grind an approximately 45° chamfer on each of the edges shown in Fig. 5.1.

From the length of 22mm diameter steel tube cut two tubes 68mm long for the steering pivot housings, tubes U and V. Ensure that the ends of the tubes are cut square.

Carry out a trial assembly of each set of components to ensure alignment of the holes – ie, assemble one of the pivot bolts, tube U and a set of stub-axle carrier parts, then similarly assemble the remaining pivot bolt with tube V and the remaining stub-axle carrier parts. When you're happy that the holes are aligned and that the all the components are satisfactory, tack-weld each set of stub-axle carrier components together – see Fig. 5.4. When tack-welding, it's a good idea to leave the pivot bolts and tubes in place to aid alignment.

Remove the pivot bolt and tube from each assembly, and fully weld both sides of each stub-axle carrier. After welding, working on each set of components in turn, re-check the alignment of the holes and the free movement of the tube by refitting the bolt and tube. If there's been some distortion, it may be possible to straighten the carrier by clamping in a vice and bending.

Fig. 5.3. The stub-axle carrier bracket assembled with the pivot bolt and tube in place.

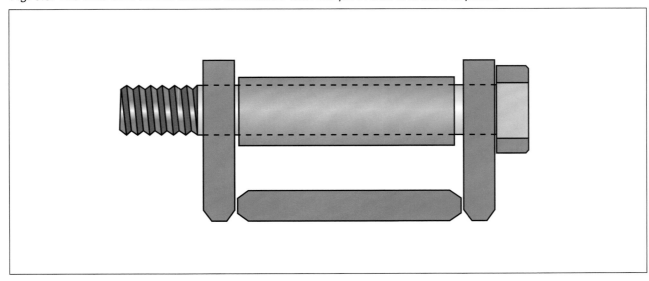

Fig. 5.4. A tack-welded stub-axle carrier showing the weld prep chamfers. (Steve Williams)

Tubes U and V can now be welded to tube D on the main frame as shown in Figs. 5.5 and 5.6. It's important to make sure that tubes U and V are welded accurately to give the correct camber and castor angles. The angle of the fish-mouthing on tube D should ensure that when tubes U and V are fitted the front wheels have a camber angle of 10° negative (ie, the tops of the wheels are inclined inwards towards the centre of the Buggy frame) and a castor angle of 15° (ie, the steering pivots are inclined forwards at the bottom). These steering angles will allow the steering to work effectively by loading up the inside front wheel during cornering, increasing its grip and helping the Buggy to turn. Although the castor angle used is high compared with that used on a car, I found that using less than 15° resulted in the Buggy having a tendency to go straight on when trying to steer left or right, and using more than 15° gave very heavy steering.

Fig. 5.5. Tubes D and U viewed from the front of the Buggy frame. Tube U should be set as shown when fixed to Tube D to give 10 degrees of negative camber.

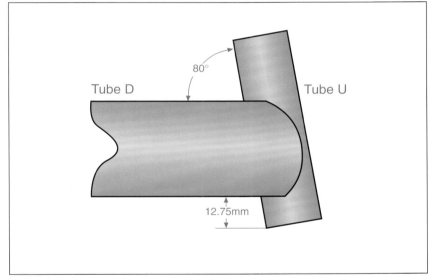

Fig. 5.6. Tubes D and U viewed from the side of the Buggy frame. Tube U should be set as shown when fixed to tube D to give a castor angle of 15 degrees.

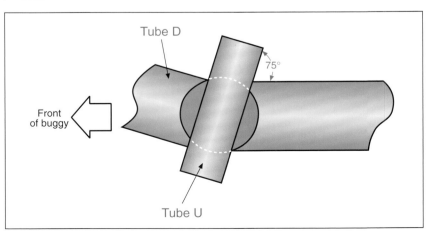

Alternative solutions

Steering pivot bolts

Instead of drilling plain holes through the top and bottom plates of each stub-axle carrier for the steering pivot bolts, you may wish to drill and tap the bottom hole to suit the thread of the pivot bolt. The bolt can then be screwed into place in the hub carrier and secured using a Nyloc nut which will act as a locknut. This solution makes it easier to adjust the tightness of the pivot bolts to ensure that the hub carriers pivot correctly.

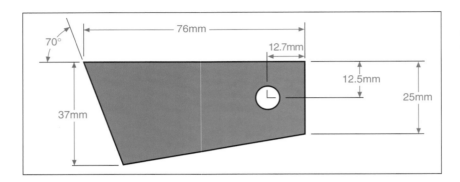

Fig. 5.7. Dimensions for the steering arms. Two steering arms are required, one for each stub-axle carrier.

MAKING THE STEERING ARMS

From the 5mm plate cut two steering arms, as shown in Fig. 5.7. The bar can be cut using a hacksaw or an electric jigsaw.

Using a centre punch, mark on each steering arm the position of the hole for the track-rod end bolt. Drill holes to suit the bolts you're going to use to secure the track-rod ends to the steering arms.

Each steering arm can now be welded to its stub-axle carrier – see Figs. 5.8 and 5.9. Remember that the stub-axle carriers are handed, so make sure that the steering arms are welded correctly to give both left- and right-handed assemblies. Also make sure that the steering arms are parallel with the top plates of the stub-axle carriers.

Fig. 5.8. A steering arm welded to the stub-axle carrier. (Steve Williams)

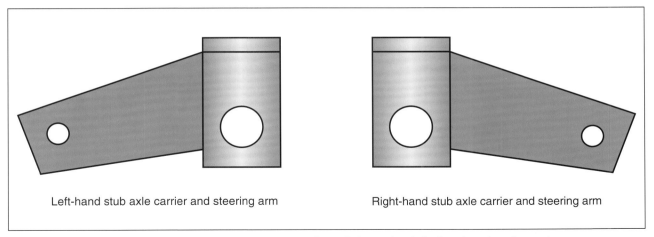

Fig. 5.9. The steering arms need to be welded on to give a left- and a right-hand stub-axle carrier.

Fig. 5.10. The front wheels and needle-roller bearings used on Derek Manders's Buggy. (Derek Manders)

MAKING THE STUB AXLES

The stub axle should be made to suit the front wheels and bearings that you intend to use on your Buggy. For my Buggy, I used four quad-bike wheels and tyres, which were bought new from a farm machinery factors. The wheels run on needle-roller bearings which are pressed into tubes welded directly to the wheels. Each wheel/bearing assembly then simply slides over the stub axle and is retained by a split-pin.

From the 25mm diameter round steel bar, or the bar which you have chosen to suit your front wheels and bearings, cut two stub axles, each 160mm long. File or grind a 10° angle on one end of each stub axle – see Fig. 5.11.

Fig. 5.11. Dimensions for stub axle. The washer needs to be welded on in the correct position for the wheels you are using.

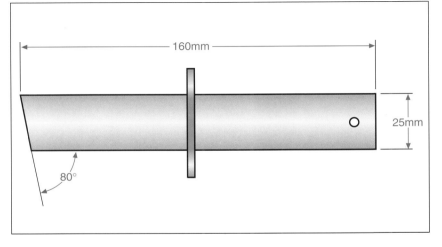

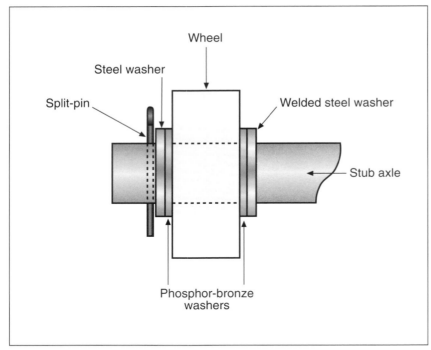

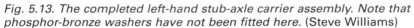

Fig. 5.12. Ideally, phosphor-bronze washers should be fitted on the stub axle either side of the wheel.

Fig. 5.13. The completed left-hand stub-axle carrier assembly. Note that phosphor-bronze washers have not been fitted here. (Steve Williams)

Weld each stub axle to the middle of the stub-axle carrier with the axle pointing down, that is, pointing away from the steering arm end of the stub-axle carrier – see Fig. 5.13.

You will now need to weld a steel washer to the inboard end of each stub axle to give the right spacing for the wheels you are going to use – the washer will act as the inner shoulder against which the wheel will rotate and, ideally, a phosphor-bronze washer should be fitted over the stub axle between the welded steel washer and the wheel. Slide the steel washer and, where applicable, the phosphor-bronze washer onto the stub axle, then slide on one of the wheels. Make sure that the rim of the wheel clears the stub-axle carrier, and also make sure that the wheel is positioned so that it will not foul the Buggy frame when the steering is turned on full lock – you may want to carry out a trial assembly of the components to check this. Once you're happy with the position of the wheel on the stub axle, mark the position of the steel washer, then remove the wheel and washers. The steel washer can now be welded onto the stub axle in the marked position, making sure that it's square with the axis of the stub axle.

Finally, you need to drill a hole in the outer end of the stub axle for the wheel retaining split-pin. Fit the inboard phosphor-bronze washer (if applicable) and the wheel to the stub axle. Ideally, a second phosphor-bronze washer should be fitted against the outer edge of the wheel, along with a second steel washer. With the wheel and washers in place, mark the required position of the split-pin hole. Depending on the type of wheel bearing you've used, the split-pin should be positioned to allow the wheel a small amount of 'float' on the stub axle, but not too much. Remove the wheel and washers, and drill the split-pin hole through the centre of the stub axle using a 3mm drill.

Ducks and dives

Welding the stub axles

On the original Buggy I welded each stub axle to the middle of its stub-axle carrier, as this meant that the Buggy sat with the frame tubes level when the wheels I chose were fitted.

One way to ensure that the stub axles are welded in the correct position is to fit the rear wheels and front stub-axle carriers to the Buggy frame, then block up the front of the Buggy frame until the side tubes are level. Attach the front wheels to the stub axles, then offer the wheels up to the frame, with the bottom of the wheels resting on the floor, and mark the positions where the stub axles need to be welded to the carriers.

MAKING THE STEERING COLUMN

Weld the head of the bolt into one end of the 19mm diameter tube being used for the steering column tube, so that the whole of the bolt thread sticks out of the end of the tube.

From the 5mm plate cut the steering column bottom bracket, as shown in Fig. 5.14, and tack-weld it to the frame in the middle of tube D.

Tack-weld the steering column support tube W (cut from the frame tube stock – see Chapter 4) in the centre of tube E, leaning towards the front of the Buggy at an angle of approximately 10° from the vertical (see Fig. 4.2 in Chapter 4). Temporarily fit the seat in the frame and trial fit the steering column. The bolt at the bottom end of the column should pass through the steering column bottom bracket on the frame. Note that when securing the column to the bottom bracket, two nuts should be

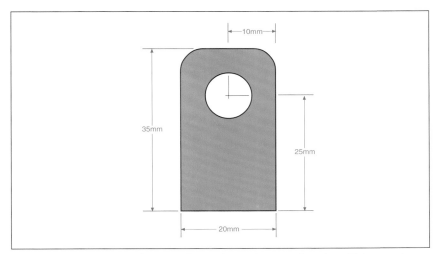

Fig. 5.14. Dimensions for steering column bottom bracket. This needs to be welded in the middle of frame Tube D.

screwed onto the end of the bolt in the column and tightened against each other – this will secure the lower end of the column, whilst still allowing it to rotate. When the column is in the best position – in other words at the correct height and angle – for the intended driver (take into account the size of the steering wheel), mark the place at which the support tube W needs to be cut. You may also need to adjust the angle of the steering column bottom bracket to suit the angle of the column – the bracket should be exactly at right-angles to the end face of the column tube.

Cut the steering column support tube at the correct angle to enable the saddle clamp to line up with the steering column, and approximately 10mm below the place marked to take account of the thickness of the saddle clamp and mounting plate.

From your 5mm plate make a

Fig. 5.15. Two nuts tightened against each other are used to secure the lower end of the steering column to the bracket on the frame. (Steve Williams)

mounting plate to suit your saddle clamp, and weld it to the top of the steering column support shaft. At the same time, you can fully weld tube W to tube E and the steering column bottom bracket to tube D.

Refit the steering column, then calculate the length it needs to be for the driver and cut to length. Remember to take into account the size of the steering wheel and mounting boss to be used.

The front stub-axle assemblies need to be fitted to the frame at this stage and a straight-edge placed across the two steering arms. Fit the stub-axle carrier assemblies to tubes U and V on the frame, and fit the steering pivot bolts to hold

them in position (if you're going to leave the components assembled for some time, fit the nuts to the steering pivot bolts). Make sure that each stub-axle carrier is fitted to the correct side of the frame – the steering arms should point towards the rear of the frame. Place the straight-edge across the steering arms, making sure that it's positioned across the centres of the holes for the track-rod end bolts at the rear of the steering arms. This will allow you to mark the position on the steering column where the straight-edge crosses the column, and gives you the centre position for the track-rod plates to be welded on the column.

From the 5mm plate, make two of the steering column track-rod plates as shown in Fig. 5.16. The plates then need to be welded either side of the marked line on the steering column, at a distance apart to suit the track-rod ends you're going to use (the two track-rod ends fit between the two plates). Make sure that the plates are welded in position at right-angles to the axis of the steering column, and make sure that the bolt holes in the plates are aligned. To check the alignment of the holes, slide the bolt you're going to use to secure the track rods to the column into position through the holes.

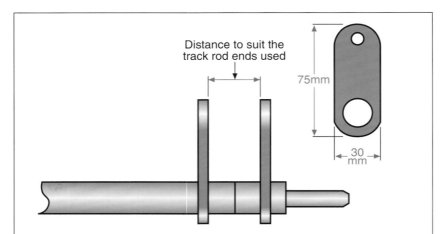

Fig. 5.16. Steering column track-rod plates. The two plates need to be welded on to the steering column at a distance apart to suit the track-rod ends you are using.

Fig. 5.17. The bottom of the steering column showing the bolt welded in place in the bottom of the tube, and the two track-rod plates in position. (Steve Williams)

Alternative solutions

Adapting a car steering column

A car steering column can be adapted for use on the Buggy, although it will almost certainly have to be shortened. Once the column has been cut to length, a bolt can be welded to the lower end to secure it, as described in the main text.

If desired, a saddle clamp can be made from solid block to suit the column from the car, and the clamp can then be secured to the Buggy frame as described in the main text. To provide positive location, the solid column can be turned down in a lathe at the appropriate place to suit the hole in the clamp (20mm in the case of the Escort column shown here).

The clamp shown here was made from a piece of 60mm x 45mm x 25mm block. The top (60mm x 25mm) face was marked out for two clamping bolts, then pilot holes were drilled, followed by drilling out to 6.8mm. On the front face (60mm x 45mm) a line was scribed across the block 20mm down from the top. The block was then sawn along this line to give two pieces. The two 6.8mm clamping bolt holes in the top piece were drilled out to 8mm, and the 6.8mm holes in the bottom piece were tapped for M8 bolts. The two pieces were then bolted together using the M8 bolts. Again working on the front face, a mark was made with a centre-punch halfway along the join, pilot drilled and then opened up to 20mm using a pillar drill.

The column and clamp can be assembled as described in the main text, and the steering wheel can be fitted using the appropriate boss for the car.

An adapted car steering column and saddle clamp. (Derek Manders)

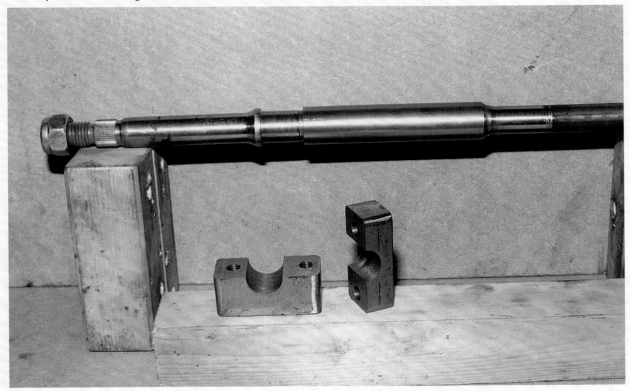

MAKING THE TRACK RODS

First, cut the 13mm diameter tube in half to give two pieces approximately 500mm long. Next weld a nut which suits the track rod ends onto one end of each of the two tubes.

Reassemble the steering column and place it in the straight-ahead position, that is, with the two steering column track-rod plates pointing straight down. Position the front stub axles in the straight-ahead position as well.

Screw a track-rod end about half-way into each of the nuts welded onto the ends of your two track rods (remember to screw a

Fig. 5.18. Track-rod inner ends secured to steering column track-rod plates. (Steve Williams)

locknut onto the threads of the track-rod end before fitting it), and then fit the bolt to secure the track-rod ends to the plates on the steering column. At this stage the required length of each track rod can be calculated by offering it up to the steering arm on the stub-axle carrier and marking on the track rod the position of the track-rod end fixing hole in the steering arm. Assuming that you're using track-rod ends at the outer ends of the track rods, remember that an allowance has to be made for the length of the track-rod end and the nut which will need welding onto the outer end of the tube once it has been cut to the required length. You should calculate the length required in order to enable the track-rod end to be screwed about half way into the track rod, leaving some exposed thread to give the possibility of adjustment later.

After cutting the track rods to the required length, you can weld the nuts onto the outer ends of the track rods, screw in the track-rod ends (again, remember to fit locknuts to the threads of the track rods before fitting), and secure the track-rod ends to the steering arms. On the original Buggy, the track-rod ends have threaded pins which are secured to the steering arms by Nyloc nuts.

Fig. 5.19. On the original Buggy, the track-rod ends have threaded pins which are secured to the steering arms by Nyloc nuts. (Paul Buckland)

Alternative solutions

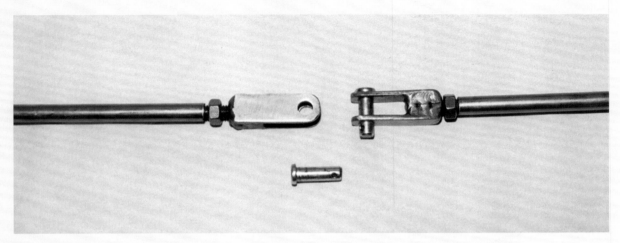

DIY track-rod ends. Note how the strips of steel plate are welded to the bolt head and nuts.
(Derek Manders)

DIY track-rod ends

If you can't find suitable proprietary track-rod ends, alternatives can be made up as follows. For each track-rod end, select a long M8 bolt, threaded along its full length, then thread two nuts onto the bolt and screw them up tight against the bolt head so that the flats on the nuts and the bolt head are aligned. Working on two opposite sides of the bolt, grind off a section from the flats of the bolt head and two nuts. Weld a strip of steel plate onto each of the ground flats, then mount the assembly in a vice and drill through the two steel plates to suit the bolts or pins to be used to secure the track-rod ends to the steering column and/or steering arms. As an alternative to using bolts, the track-rod ends can be secured to the steering arms using clevis-pins and split-pins.

Before fitting each track-rod end, screw a lock nut onto the bolt thread, then screw the bolt thread into the end of the track rod. After final assembly, the lengths of the track rods can be adjusted, and the lock nuts can then be tightened.

Note that if rose-jointed track-rod ends are not used, it will be necessary to bend the steering arms very slightly so that the bolt/pin holes in the steering arms and track-rod ends are aligned (rose joints can cope with this slight misalignment).

Note also that as the track rods need to pivot to a significant degree, it would be unwise to use DIY track-rod ends at both ends of the track rods. To avoid the risk of overstressing the pivots, it is advisable to use rose-jointed track-rod ends at the inboard (steering column) ends of the track rods.

DIY track-rod end connected to steering arm using a clevis-pin and split-pin. (Steve Williams)

FITTING THE STEERING WHEEL

Finally, weld a boss to the top of the steering column to allow your chosen steering wheel to be securely attached. In many cases a suitable boss will be supplied with your steering wheel. As an alternative, if you use a steering wheel from a scrap car, you could salvage the car steering column, saw off the top splined section, and weld it to the top of the Buggy column. The steering wheel can then be attached to the column using the original nut or bolt from the car. On the original Buggy I used a quick-release steering wheel, and welded the boss supplied to the top of the column.

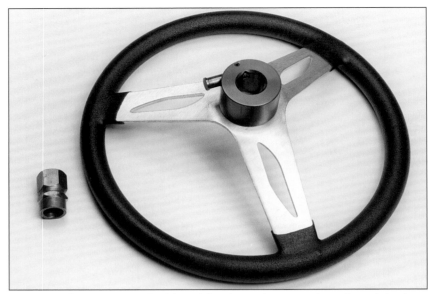

Fig. 5.20. Steering wheel with quick-release boss used on the original Buggy. Any steering wheel can be used provided it can be securely fixed to the steering column. (Steve Williams)

Chapter 6
The engine and gearbox

The exact way in which the engine/gearbox assembly is mounted will of course depend on the engine/gearbox being used. Although actually installing the engine/gearbox is a fairly straightforward task, it's important to make sure that all the controls are correctly connected and adjusted before using the Buggy.

WHAT YOU NEED

Tools required

Welding set
Welding mask or goggles, gloves, overalls and safety boots
Steel tape measure
Steel ruler and set square
Hacksaw
Files – one flat, one round
Wire brush
Electric drill with a selection of drill bits
Socket set
Set of ring spanners
Set of open-ended spanners
Set of Allen keys
Centre punch

Materials required

5mm steel plate – can be cut from remainder of sheet used during frame construction
Selection of nuts, bolts and washers to suit components removed from donor motorcycle
Suffolk Colt lawnmower fuel tank, complete with on/off tap, fuel pipe and vented screw cap
Two hose clips to suit fuel pipe
Engine and gearbox (complete with carburettor, ignition system, exhaust system and clutch)

FITTING THE ENGINE AND GEARBOX

Refit the engine/gearbox assembly to your frame, and bolt securely to the mounting plates welded in place when you made the frame.

The fuel tank needs positioning above the carburettor, as most older small-capacity motorcycle engines do not have fuel pumps and rely on gravity to feed fuel to the engine. For safety's sake you need an on/off tap on the fuel tank, or in the fuel feed pipe, and a screw-on ventilated fuel tank cap. I found all these features came as standard with the lawnmower fuel tank I'd purchased.

On the original Buggy, the tank was fitted to the frame by fabricating a suitable bracket out of the 5mm plate and welding it to the frame on tube L. I also had to weld a bolt to the frame to secure the fuel tank top mounting bracket. Some lawnmower fuel tanks are designed to be mounted on the mower handle tubes, in which case you can mount the tank on the Buggy by welding a suitably bent tube to the frame.

Once the tank is in position on the bracket, fit the fuel feed pipe

Fig. 6.1. The petrol tank on the original Buggy, showing the simple bracket made to fix it in position on the frame tube. Note also the bolt which secures the tank's top bracket. (Steve Williams)

from the tank to the carburettor, making sure that the pipe is secure and held clear of any moving parts with which it could tangle. Secure the pipe with a hose clip at each end.

With the Yamaha 175cc engine I fitted, it was necessary to make a slight modification to the exhaust pipe so that it would exit to the back of the Buggy. A single cut was made, on the outlet pipe near the cylinder head, to allow the silencer and tail pipe to be rotated. The pipe was then re-welded. An important point to note if your engine is a 2-stroke unit is that the overall length and internal volume of the exhaust pipe for a 2-stroke engine is precisely calculated and designed to ensure that the engine runs properly. On no account should the length of the exhaust be changed.

Fix the exhaust to the engine and, if necessary, make up a bracket or brackets to support the exhaust and attach it to a suitable frame tube such as tube H.

Fig. 6.2. An alternative type of lawnmower fuel tank mounted on a bent tube welded to the Buggy frame. (Derek Manders)

Fig. 6.3. The exhaust was cut, rotated and re-welded so it exited at the back of the buggy. We were careful not to change the length or volume of the exhaust. (Steve Williams)

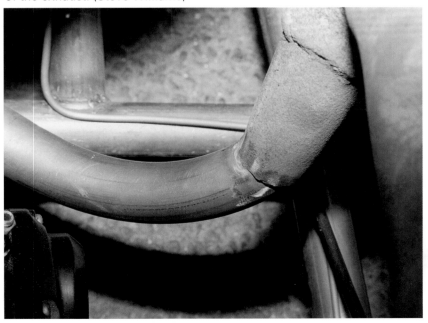

Fig. 6.4. On the original Buggy two brackets were welded to the frame to mount the exhaust. (Steve Williams)

Fig. 6.5. The Honda 70 engine/gearbox installation on Derek Manders's Buggy. (Steve Williams)

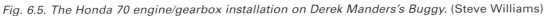

Ducks and dives

Exhaust heat shield

Having completed the Buggy illustrated in this book, whilst running the engine, I was leaning across and accidentally burnt a running hole in my new trousers. She who must be obeyed was not amused! One of the first modifications will be a heat shield, probably made from perforated aluminium, which will protect skin – far more precious than trousers!

Ducks and dives

2-stroke petrol/oil mix

Some 2-stroke engines have a separate oil tank, with a device on the engine which automatically feeds in the correct mix of oil and petrol. On some motorcycles the tubular frame itself is used as an oil tank. If your donor motorcycle uses two tanks, you have two options. Either fit two separate tanks, or mix the oil and petrol in the correct proportions before filling the fuel tank – the original manufacturer of the motorcycle will give the required proportions.

  If you're using an oil/petrol mix in the fuel tank, then the oil and petrol can separate out if the Buggy is not used for some time. If your Buggy has been stood for a while, give it a shake to mix the oil and petrol before you try and start it. Always make sure that the two-stroke oil/petrol mix is correct.

  If a two-stoke petrol/oil mix is used in the fuel tank, instead of an auto-feed petrol/oil system, it would be as well to check whether the oil supply pipes need blocking off and/or whether the oil pump needs to be removed to avoid air being pumped into the engine. I do know that this was necessary on some Japanese bikes that I worked on years ago. This is where a *Haynes Service and Repair Manual* would come in handy.

This is what happens if you use too much oil in a two-stroke oil/petrol mix – smoke! (Steve Williams)

Chapter 7

Drivetrain and brake

As with the other components of the Buggy, it's important to make sure that work on the drivetrain and brake components is carried out safely and accurately. Don't try to improvise as far as rear axle and brake component mountings are concerned, as the safety of the driver is at stake. If you're lucky enough to succeed in obtaining any proprietary kart components for use on your Buggy (eg, rear axle, wheels hubs, etc), always follow the manufacturer's recommendations for fitting.

WHAT YOU NEED

Tools required

Welding set
Welding mask or goggles, gloves, overalls and safety boots
Steel tape measure
Steel ruler and set square
Hacksaw
Files – one flat, one round
Wire brush
Electric drill with a selection of drill bits
Socket set
Set of ring spanners
Set of open-ended spanners
Access to a metalworking lathe
Screwdrivers

Materials required

Chain, sprockets, front brake disc and front brake caliper from donor motorcycle
Four Ford differential flanges (on my Buggy these came from Ford Capris)
2 self-centring bearings for rear axle

1000mm length of 30mm diameter solid steel bar – for rear axle*
5mm steel plate – can be cut from remainder of sheet used during frame construction
38mm diameter tube off-cut – for gear linkage support
Selection of nuts, bolts and washers to suit components removed from donor motorcycle
Chain oil
3 off M6 or M8 bolts and self-locking nuts to secure drive sprocket flange and wheel hub flanges to axle – optional (see text)
* The rear axle on the original Buggy was made from 30mm solid bar steel stock. When buying material to make the axle, take advice from the stockholder – hard steel must be used, not malleable

steel, as if the axle is malleable, it may bend after rigorous off-road use. Proprietary axles can be bought from karting specialists, in which case bearings and wheel mounting flanges can be bought to suit, although this is likely to be a more expensive option than making your own axle. Kart axles are designed to withstand the rigours of karting, so should be perfectly adequate for the Buggy.

MACHINING THE HUBS

If you have access to a metal-working lathe, bore out the centres of the four differential flanges to fit the axle shaft. If you don't have access to a lathe, a local

Fig. 7.1. The rear differential flange obtained from a scrap Ford Capri. (Steve Williams)

Fig. 7.2. The Ford rear differential flanges will need to be machined to suit the rear axle, sprocket, brake disc and wheels you are going to use. (Steve Williams)

Fig. 7.3. Proprietary hubs can be obtained from go-kart specialist suppliers, but are likely to be quite expensive. (Steve Williams)

engineering shop can easily do this.

One of the hubs needs to be fitted to the sprocket. Either the flange can be drilled to fit the holes already in the sprocket or the sprocket can be drilled to fit the holes in the flange.

A second flange needs to be fitted to the brake disc – again the flange can be drilled to fit the holes already in the sprocket or the sprocket can be drilled to fit the holes in the flange.

The remaining two flanges must be drilled to suit the pitch circle diameter (PCD) of the rear wheels to be used – in other words the flanges must be drilled to accept the wheel fixing bolts. It goes without saying that you need to make sure that the holes drilled are concentric with the flange and the wheel. For my Buggy I was fortunate to be given two proprietary aluminium go-kart hubs, but not many builders will be this lucky and these hubs are rather expensive to buy new.

Bolt the drive sprocket and the brake disc to their respective flanges.

FITTING THE BRAKE DISC AND CALIPER

When mounting the brake disc and caliper, note that the caliper will probably have been designed to work with the disc rotating in a specific direction. When mounting the disc and caliper on the Buggy, make sure that the caliper is mounted so that it operates with the disc rotating in the same direction as it did when fitted to the donor motorcycle.

Loosely bolt the two self-centring bearings into the axle bearing mounting plates on the frame, then slide the axle shaft through one of the bearings. Slide the brake disc and drive sprocket onto the axle, before sliding the axle through the second bearing on the opposite side. Finally, slide on the two wheel hubs.

With the axle positioned centrally in the frame, the brake

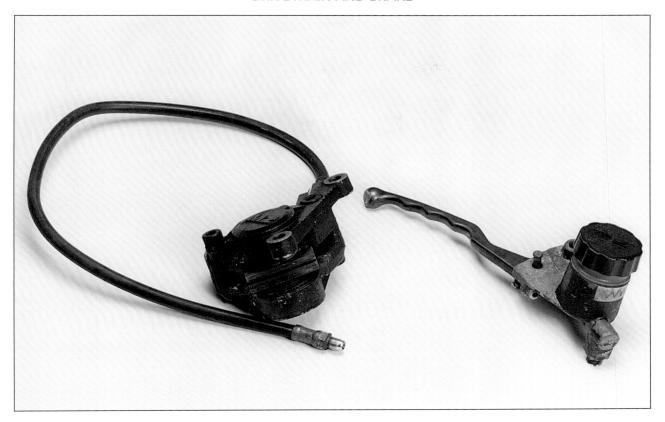

Fig. 7.4. The brake master cylinder and caliper from the donor motorcycle. It's unlikely that the flexible brake pipe will be suitable for use on the Buggy. (Steve Williams)

Fig. 7.5. One of the two proprietary self-centring bearings we bought for the rear axle of the buggy. The inside diameter of the bearing must match the axle you intend to use. (Steve Williams)

Fig. 7.6. The bearing, axle and hub assembled on the completed Buggy. (Paul Buckland)

disc can be slid along until it's positioned close to a frame tube that will provide a firm location for the bracket to be used to support the caliper. On the original Buggy, I welded a bracket to frame tube B.

With the brake disc in position on the axle, and the axle in place in the frame, offer up the brake caliper to the disc and measure the distance from the appropriate frame tube to the caliper. This will enable you to design a suitable bracket to hold the caliper in the correct position. For my bracket I used an off-cut from the 38mm tube used to make the frame, along with two strips of 5mm plate. The strips of plate were welded to the end of the tube off-cut, and holes were drilled in the plate to suit the caliper mounting bolts. The caliper and disc where then moved out of the way, and the bracket was tack-welded to frame tube B.

With the caliper mounting bracket tack-welded to the frame, the disc and caliper can be moved back into position, and the caliper can be bolted to its bracket.

Once the caliper has been firmly bolted into position, mark the position of the disc-mounting flange on the axle shaft.

FITTING THE DRIVE SPROCKET AND WHEEL HUBS

Place a straight-edge against the end face of the drive sprocket on the engine/gearbox, and use it to position the drive sprocket on the axle. It's critical that the two sprockets run exactly in line, because if there is any misalignment the Buggy will continuously throw the chain. Once you're happy that the sprockets are aligned, mark the position of the drive-sprocket flange on the axle.

Bolt your chosen rear wheels to the hub flanges, then slide them onto the axle to give the desired track width. The wheels should be positioned with between 15 and 20mm clearance between the inside edge of the tyre and the Buggy frame. Again mark the position of the hub flanges on the axle.

Unbolt the bearings from the axle bearing mounting plates on the frame, then remove the bearings and axle, and cut off any excess length that protrudes beyond the hub flanges at each end of the axle. The brake disc and flange can now be placed back on the axle in the marked position and fully welded to the axle. At the same time, you should also fully weld the brake caliper support bracket to the frame.

You now have to take a decision on how to fix the drive sprocket and the wheel hubs to the axle. The flanges can be welded to the axle, or they can be secured using bolts. If bolts are used, each bolt will act as a shear pin which should break if excessive load is applied to the drivetrain, preventing serious damage to the engine/gearbox.

Fig. 7.7. I made the caliper mounting bracket from two pieces of 5mm plate welded to an off-cut of the 38mm frame tube. This was then welded to frame tube B. (Steve Williams)

The choice is up to you, but if you decide to use bolts, don't be tempted to fit larger than 8mm bolts as this will weaken the axle as well as providing less protection against overloading the drivetrain, and don't be tempted to secure the brake disc flange to the axle using a bolt – this could result in no braking just when you need it most! I strongly recommend that you use bolts to secure the wheel hub flanges, as if the flanges are welded to the axle, you'll have problems if you need to change the wheel bearings, or indeed if you decide to use wheels with a different PCD (possibly needing new hubs), at a later date. If you do decide to weld the wheel hub flanges to the axle, make sure that you slide the bearings onto the axle first – you will not be able to fit them once the flanges have been welded in position!

When you've decided on your chosen method of securing the drive sprocket flange and wheel hub flanges to the axle, either fully weld them in position, or secure them with bolts as follows. With the drive sprocket and hubs removed from the axle, drill holes through the flanges for the fixing bolts. Place the flanges in their correct positions on the axle and, using the holes already drilled in the flanges as a guide, drill through the axle. Make sure that the bolts are long enough to pass all the way through both sides of the flange, leaving sufficient thread exposed to fit the nuts.

Fig. 7.8. The completed brake disc and caliper assembly fitted to the Buggy. (Steve Williams)

Reassemble the axle with the drive sprocket and bearings. Slip the motorcycle drive chain onto the axle before refitting the axle and bearings in the frame. Tighten the bearing fixing bolts, then check that the axle rotates freely in the bearings.

On the original Buggy, the axle is prevented from moving from side to side in the bearings by using grub screws, threaded through holes in the bearing inner races, which engage with indentations in the axle. If you have similar bearings to the ones I used, and you want to use this method of locating the axle, you need to make sure that the grub screws locate securely. With the axle in position on the Buggy, tighten the grub screws to make marks on the surface of the axle. Remove the axle and drill shallow indentations in its surface to provide locations for the grub screws. Refit the axle, then apply a little thread-locking compound to the threads of the grub screws, and

tighten them securely, making sure that they engage with the indentations in the axle.

FITTING THE CHAIN

You'll find that the chain from the donor motorcycle will be too long for the Buggy, as the engine/gearbox is mounted much nearer to the drive sprocket than it was on the motorcycle. With the chain fitted over both the engine and axle sprockets, work out the required length of the chain, and calculate how many chain links need to be removed. You'll probably need to remove the axle and chain again to split the chain and remove links. This can usually be done using a hammer and punch to knock out the chain-link pins. If you're having difficulty, your local motorcycle dealer/ repairer should have the special tools required to do it for you.

Once your chain is the right length, slip it over the axle and refit

the axle and bearings, remembering to make sure that the chain is correctly fitted round both the engine/gearbox and axle sprockets before the bearings are bolted to the support plates on the frame. Where applicable, align the fixing bolt holes in the sprocket and wheel hub flanges with those in the axle, and fit and tighten the fixing bolts and nuts.

Lubricate the chain well with chain lubricant available from motorcycle accessory and repair shops.

If you've incorporated a method of chain adjustment into the design of your Buggy, either by means of adjusting the position of the engine/gearbox or the rear axle, now is the time to make the adjustment. Take care not to over-tension the chain, as this will cause excessive wear of the chain and sprockets.

Finally, if you haven't done so already, fit the hubs and wheels to the Buggy.

Fig. 7.9. The sprockets and drive chain in position. You're likely to have to shorten the chain to suit your Buggy. (Steve Williams)

Chapter 8
Controls and starting devices

The Buggy is controlled much like a car, rather than a motorcycle, with three pedals, one for the accelerator, one for the clutch and one for the brake. We therefore have to modify the controls to suit. When building the original Buggy, I decided to keep all the controls very simple, and therefore straightforward and cheap to make. There's plenty of scope for customising the components here, adding your own individual touches to, for instance, the pedal and gear-change designs.

WHAT YOU NEED

Tools required

Welding set
Welding mask or goggles, gloves, overalls and safety boots
Steel tape measure
Steel ruler and set square
Files – one flat, one round
Wire brush
Electric drill with a selection of drill bits
Socket set
Set of ring spanners
Set of open-ended spanners
Hammer
Pliers/wire cutters
Brake pipe flaring tool

Materials required

2000mm length of 20mm x 5mm flat steel bar – for pedals and gear-change linkage*
Length of steel tube to fit from gear-change splined shaft on gearbox to outer frame tube – see text
Hand-brake and master cylinder from donor motorcycle
Selection of nuts, bolts and washers
2m of 3/16in copper brake pipe and suitable fittings
Assorted tension springs (to use as pedal return springs)
Clutch cable from car – see text
Accelerator cable from car – see text
Cable ties
**While you can use 5mm plate for these parts, securing flat bar will reduce the amount of cutting required.*

If you're using an engine with electric start in your Buggy, you'll need to take the associated wiring, a battery, and ideally an acid-proof battery box from the donor motorcycle.

PEDALS

From the 20mm x 5mm flat bar, make 3 pedal blanks as shown in Fig. 8.1 and then cut and bend them, as shown, in a vice to produce the three pedals required. The cut should be made along the bend line to aid bending, but take care not to make the cut too deep.

Fig. 8.1. You can make the pedals to suit your requirement. These are the dimensions of the ones I made. The two small holes are for the return springs.

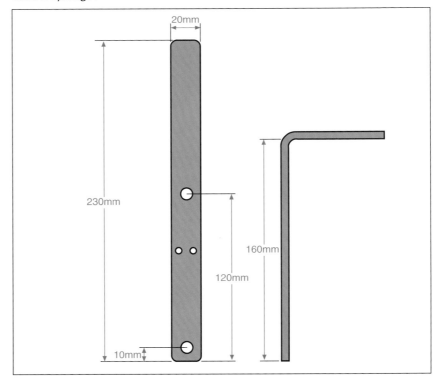

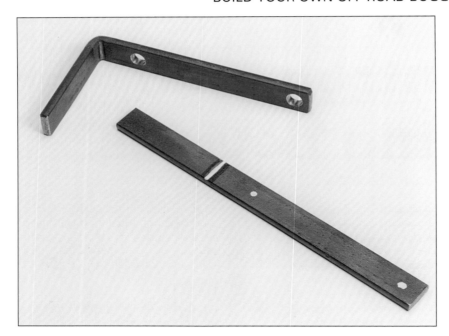

Fig. 8.2. After marking out and cutting the pedal blank it can be bent over at 90 degrees using a vice and hammer. (Steve Williams)

The pedals are fixed to the frame by welding bolts to tubes N, O and P in positions to suit the length of the driver's legs, and to give the necessary pedal movement. A back-stop should be fitted to prevent each pedal from moving too far back, and to position the pedals correctly for the driver's feet. These back-stops can be made from surplus tube, plate, another bolt or round bar, as shown in Fig. 8.3. When you've welded the pedal mounting bolts and back-stops in place, the pedals can be fitted to the frame ready for the cables to be attached.

It's a good idea to fit a return spring to each of the three pedals, and it's essential for the accelerator pedal. Drill a hole in the pedal to take one end of the spring, and a washer can be welded to the frame to secure the other end – see Fig. 8.3.

Bear in mind that the higher the cable attachment up the pedal, the greater the leverage and the less the effort will be required to operated the brakes, clutch or accelerator.

Fig. 8.3. A return spring and stop should be used on each pedal to give a better 'feel' and positive action. In this photograph you can see the method by which the spring has been attached to the frame tube, and the round bar welded to the frame to make the pedal stop. (Steve Williams)

Alternative solutions

Pedals

More substantial pedal mountings can be made by drilling through the frame tubes and welding in a length of thick-walled 8mm tube, through which the pedal pivot bolts are passed. The main pedal arms themselves can be made from 25mm angle, with a piece of tube welded in place to accept the pivot bolt. For the finishing touch, race-style pedal pads can be fastened to the pedals.

An alternative arrangement for the pedals. Lengths of thick-walled 8mm tube have been welded into the frame tubes to carry the pivot bolts. Note also the brackets with nuts welded to them to carry the pedal-stop bolts. (Derek Manders)

For the finishing touch, race-style pedal pads have been added. (Derek Manders)

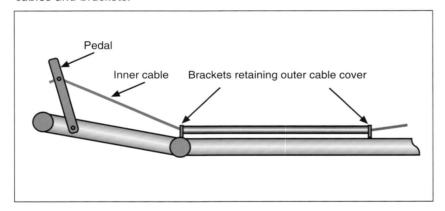

Fig. 8.4. This is typical of the mounting brackets you will require to fit the control cables. The hole in the bracket should be large enough to let the inner cable pass through easily but smaller than the diameter of the cable sheath.

Fig. 8.5. This is a schematic view of how you should set-up your control cables and brackets.

SOURCING THE CONTROL CABLES

The control cables from the donor motorcycle are generally too light duty to cope with being used with a foot pedal, as they're only intended for hand use. To avoid the problems of snapped cables, for my Buggy I obtained car clutch and accelerator cables which are heavier duty. Make sure the cables you obtain are long enough and that the outer sheathing is long enough to fit between the support brackets which you will weld to the frame near to the pedals and the engine/gearbox. You may decide to use suitable 'off-the-shelf' Bowden cable (such as cycle brake cable) rather than car cables, but make sure that whatever you use is up to the job.

MOUNTING BRACKETS

From the 5mm flat bar (or plate) make 4, 5 or 6 mounting brackets as shown in Fig. 8.4. The number you require depends on whether suitable brackets already exist on the engine/gearbox for the accelerator and clutch cables. The holes for the cables in the brackets should be drilled at a size which allows the inner cables you are going to use to pass through, but smaller than the diameter of the cable sheathing.

Alternative solutions

Securing the control cables

To keep the control cables tidy and secure on the Buggy frame, in addition to the cable mounting brackets, short lengths of tube can be welded to the frame and the cable can then be fed through the tubes.

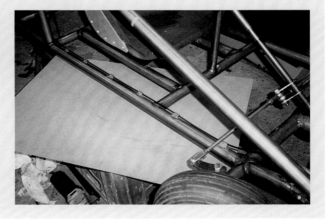

Here, short lengths of tube have been welded to the frame, and the accelerator cable has been fed through the tubes. (Derek Manders)

Fig. 8.6. Drill the hand-brake lever on the motorcycle brake master cylinder to take the brake operating cable. I left the handle in place for emergency operation of the brake. (Steve Williams)

BRAKE MASTER CYLINDER AND CABLE

Fig. 8.7. An alternative method of fixing the brake operating cable to the hand-brake lever. (Derek Manders)

From the 5mm plate, make up a bracket to mount the motorcycle brake master cylinder and hand-brake lever at the bottom of the steering support tube W. Drill the plate to suit the master cylinder and lever mountings, then weld the plate in position on the frame. Note that when fitted to the Buggy, the master cylinder fluid reservoir should be upright – if this is not possible, make sure that the reservoir cap has a good seal to prevent fluid spillage.

Weld one of the cable mounting plates to the frame tube E, then weld another plate to tube D in line with the brake foot pedal.

Drill a hole big enough for the inner brake cable to pass through in

Fig. 8.8. The cable is fixed to the pedal using a bolt, two washers and two nuts. The nut holding the cable should be tight, but the other should be left slightly loose to allow the bolt to rotate. (Steve Williams)

the hand-brake lever approximately 25mm from its pivot point.

There may already be a ball or other end fitting swaged onto the end of the cable you're using – if so this can be used to prevent the cable pulling through the drilled hand-brake lever. If not, a cable end fitting can be made using a drilled-through bolt, a nut and two washers. Put one of the washers on the bolt and then drill a hole through the bolt, as close as possible to the washer, big enough for the inner cable to pass through. Feed the cable through the hole in the bolt and fit the second washer, then clamp the cable by screwing the nut tightly up against the second washer.

Thread the cable through the hand-brake lever and through the mounting bracket as shown in Fig. 8.6. Slide the outer sheath onto the cable – this needs to be long enough to fit tightly between the mounting bracket on tube E and the mounting bracket on tube D in line with the brake pedal. Cut the cable sheath to length if necessary.

The cable is secured to the pedal by a bolt, 2 nuts (one Nyloc) and two washers. Put one of the washers on the bolt, and then drill a hole through the bolt, as close as possible to the washer, big enough for the inner cable to pass through. Feed the cable through the hole in the bolt and fit the second washer. Run the first nut up the bolt and tighten it against the washer to securely clamp the cable. Put the bolt through the hole in the pedal and secure using the Nyloc nut, but do not tighten down – the bolt needs to be free to rotate as the pedal is operated.

Rather than cut off the hand-brake lever, I left it in place so that it would be available for emergency hand operation of the brake if the cable ever snapped.

ACCELERATOR CABLE

The accelerator cable is fitted in much the same way as the brake cable. At the carburettor end the cable is threaded through the carburettor throttle lever. If necessary, weld a cable mounting bracket to a suitable frame member to retain the cable outer sheath. You may find that there's a suitable bracket already in position on the engine which was used for the original cable.

Weld another cable mounting bracket in line with the accelerator pedal on frame tube D. Thread the accelerator cable through the throttle lever on the carburettor (if necessary make up a cable end fitting, as described for the brake cable), through the bracket at the carburettor end, and then slip on the outer sheath and cut to length if necessary to get a good fit between the bracket at the carburettor end and the bracket on tube D. Thread the inner cable through the bracket on tube D and fix to the accelerator pedal as described for the brake cable.

CLUTCH CABLE

The clutch cable is attached in the same way as the brake and accelerator cables. One end of the inner cable is first attached to the clutch actuating arm at the engine/gearbox. Again you may find that there's a suitable bracket already in position on the engine, otherwise weld a cable mounting bracket to a suitable tube on the frame, or it may be necessary to fit a bracket to a suitable location on the engine/gearbox.

Weld a cable mounting bracket in line with the clutch pedal on frame tube D. Thread the clutch cable through the bracket at the engine/gearbox end, fit the outer sheath and cut to length if necessary to get a good fit between the bracket at the engine/gearbox end and the bracket on tube D. Thread the inner cable through the bracket in tube D, and fix to the clutch pedal as described previously for the other cables. The clutch cable I used has the advantage of a screw thread on the pedal end of the cable. I designed a modified pedal fixing for the cable by welding a nut with a suitable thread onto a bolt through the pedal – see Fig. 8.9. This means that there is an easy method of adjusting the clutch cable.

Fig. 8.9. Because the clutch cable we used had a screw thread on one end, I adapted the fixing to give a more easily adjustable cable. (Steve Williams)

BRAKE HYDRAULIC PIPE

You'll need to run a length of hydraulic pipe from the brake caliper to the motorcycle brake master cylinder which you've fixed to the frame. It's likely that the donor motorcycle had a flexible pipe which is too short for using on the Buggy. It's cheaper and safer to use copper or steel brake pipe in place of the flexible pipe.

Brake pipes have a special flare and fitting on either end. Brake pipe flaring tools can be purchased, but for the single pipe you require for your Buggy it's cheaper to have the flaring done by a local garage. Measure the length of pipe required, remembering it's wise to route the pipe along the frame tubes for protection. For example, you may wish to run the pipe along tubes R, F and B, so allow extra length for this. Take the old flexible pipe from the

motorcycle with you, so the garage can see what thread size and what type of flare is required at each end of the new pipe.

Once you have a brake pipe of the correct length, with the end fittings in place, you can gently bend the pipe by hand to give the required shape. Take care not to kink the pipe, as this will restrict the fluid flow and prevent the brake from working properly. When the pipe is the right shape, screw the end fittings into the master cylinder and caliper, and secure the pipe to the frame tubes at intervals with cable ties.

Once the pipe and all the components are secured, you can fill the fluid reservoir on the master cylinder with the correct hydraulic fluid and bleed the system to remove air. The relevant workshop manual for you donor motorcycle should give details of the bleeding procedure. When you're bleeding the system, make sure that the

master cylinder is higher than the caliper, to avoid trapping air in the system – tilt the Buggy and support it on an axle stand if necessary.

GEAR CHANGE

Unlike a car, the gear change on a motorcycle is foot operated and sequential. The gear-change pedal normally has an internally splined split boss, which fits on a splined shaft from the gearbox. The boss is clamped down onto the shaft using a pinch-bolt. For the Buggy, the gear change needs to be adapted to hand operation.

Start by removing the gear-change pedal boss from the pedal by hacksawing it off – see Fig. 8.12. Cut a length of steel tube, of a diameter to suit the gearbox splined shaft (in my case 19mm diameter – I used an off-cut from the steering column tube), of sufficient length to reach from the splined shaft to the outer frame

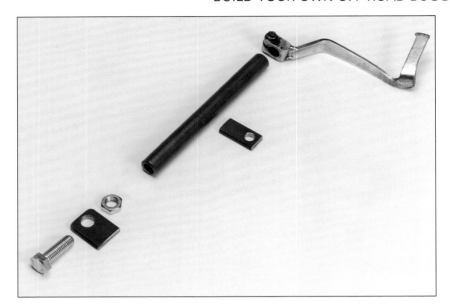

Fig. 8.10. The parts required to make the gear-change shaft. (Steve Williams)

Fig. 8.11. The splined split boss from the donor motorcycle, showing it welded to the gear-change pedal. (Steve Williams)

Fig. 8.12. Remove the boss from the pedal using a hacksaw. (Steve Williams)

tube A or B. The side of the engine/transmission from which the splined shaft exits will determine on which side of the Buggy you fit the gear-change. In one end of the tube cut a slot approximately 30mm long and 3mm wide to match the slot in the splined boss removed from the pedal, then weld the boss onto the end of the tube with the slots lined up. The slot is to allow the end of the tube to close down as the pinch-bolt in the boss is tightened.

The gear-change tube will be secured at the outer end by a bolt, which will pass through a bracket welded to the Buggy frame, and screw into a nut welded to the end of the tube.

From your 5mm bar or plate, make a mounting bracket similar to the one shown in Fig. 8.13 to support the outer end of the gear-change tube. This bracket will be welded to the top of the outer frame tube A or B, and the position of the hole must be such that the gear-change tube is horizontal

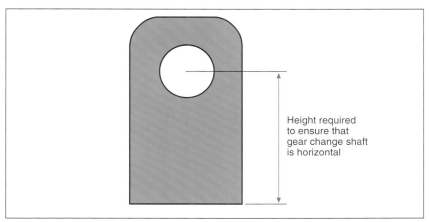

Height required to ensure that gear change shaft is horizontal

Fig. 8.13. You'll have to adapt this basic bracket to give the required height to make sure that the gear-change tube is horizontal.

when bolted in position. Weld your mounting bracket to the frame tube in the correct position, then cut the gear-change tube to the required length, so that with the splined boss in the end of the tube fitted over the end of the gearbox splined shaft, the gear-change tube reaches the bracket on the outer frame tube. When cutting the tube, allow for the width of the nut which

will be welded onto the end of the tube to secure it to the bracket on the frame. With the tube cut to length, weld the nut onto the outer end of the tube.

Now make up a gear-change link bracket and weld it to the gear-change tube. This bracket should be long enough to make sure that the gear-change link will clear frame tube F, and should be

Fig. 8.14. Gear-change tube splined boss fitted over the end of the gearbox splined shaft. (Steve Williams)

Fig. 8.15. *The gear-change lever assembly in position on the Buggy frame.* (Steve Williams)

Fig. 8.16. *The gear-change link in position between the gear-change lever and the gear-change tube.* (Steve Williams)

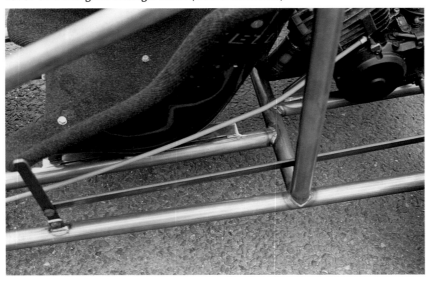

positioned sufficiently 'inboard' on the gear-change tube to ensure that the link clears the frame roll-bar tube K – see Fig. 8.16. The link bracket will have to be drilled at its top end for the link bolt.

Again from the 5mm plate or bar, make a mounting bracket for the gear-change lever, and cut a length for the gear-change lever itself. The bracket should be similar in style to that shown in Fig. 8.13. The lever should be of a length that is comfortable for the intended driver, with a hole in the lower end to allow it to be bolted to the bracket on the frame, and second hole to allow it to be bolted to the gear-change link – see Fig. 8.15.

Mark the desired position of the gear-change lever support bracket on the frame, then weld the bracket to the frame. Bolt the gear-change lever to the bracket, and secure it with a Nyloc nut – see Fig. 8.15. Do not tighten the nut hard against the lever, as you have to be able to move the lever freely.

Fit the inner end of the gear-change tube to the gearbox splined shaft, with the link bracket on the tube positioned vertically up, and bolt the outer end of the tube to the bracket on the frame. Make sure that the gear-change lever is in the vertical position, then measure the distance between the gear-change lever and the link bracket on the gear-change tube to determine the required length of the link. Make the link out of 5mm flat bar, and bolt it into position between the gear-change lever and the link bracket on the tube, using bolts and Nyloc nuts – again do not overtighten the nuts, as there must be free movement.

Fit the pinch-bolt to the boss on the gearbox splined shaft, and tighten it. Check that there is free movement of the gear-change linkage backwards and forwards. Once the Buggy is completed, you can check that all the gears can be engaged, and the gear-change linkage can be adjusted if necessary by altering the position of the boss (and tube) on the splines of the gearbox shaft.

Alternative solutions

Gear-change lever

As an alternative to a simple gear-change lever made from steel plate or bar, a lever can be made from 20mm box-section steel, with a hole drilled through the bottom to accept a steel tube through which the pivot bolt can pass. To make the lever look even more professional, a bolt can be welded to the top to accept a plastic gear knob.

Gear-change lever support

A more substantial gear-change lever mounting can be made by drilling through the frame tube and welding in a length of thick-walled 8mm tube, through which the lever pivot bolt is passed. A short length of bar welded to frame tube E will provide additional support for the lever.

Gear-change linkage

If a Honda 70 engine is used, a simple gear linkage can be made by removing the gear-change pedal from its shaft on

the engine/gearbox, then cutting it down using a hacksaw, and flattening it in a vice. The pedal can then be refitted to its shaft in a vertical position, with a hole drilled towards the bottom to accept a 6mm bolt. A gear-change link rod can be made from steel tube with a nut welded to each end, as described for the track rods in Chapter 5. Two end fittings can be made from steel strip, with an 8mm hole drilled through the centre into which an 8mm bolt can be welded. The end fittings should be bent into a U-shape to suit the gear-change lever and the gear-change pedal on the engine/gearbox, and then drilled to suit the bolt or clevis pin to be used to secure them to the lever and pedal. Locknuts can then be screwed onto the end fitting bolts, and the end fittings can be screwed into the ends of the link rod. The end fittings can be screwed in or out of the link rod as required for adjustment, and then connected to the lever and pedal using bolts and Nyloc nuts, or clevis pins and split-pins.

An alternative design of gear-change lever made from box-section steel. (Steve Williams)

A short length of bar welded to the frame will provide additional support for the lever. (Steve Williams)

A simple gear-change linkage arrangement for the Honda 70 engine/gearbox. (Steve Williams)

STARTING

The engine fitted to my Buggy was designed to be started using a kick-start. However, when the engine is fitted to the Buggy, the space in which to operate that kick-start is limited. I've described how I started the Buggy in 'The original Buggy design' at the beginning of Chapter 3.

For shear luxury, if you have sourced a later model motorcycle as a donor, it will probably have an electric start. This does mean that you will have to carry a battery fitted in a suitable position, probably behind the driver's seat. You'll also need to install the necessary wiring and fit a start button which can be easily reached by the driver when seated in the normal position. If you're using an electric start, find an acid-proof battery box – the donor motorcycle will probably have one – which will prevent the possibility of an acid spill injuring the driver or damaging the Buggy if the Buggy is being driven over rough ground or up steep slopes, etc.

Ducks and dives

Lubrication

Lubricate all the control cables with WD40 or a similar lubricant. This is particularly important if your Buggy is used in wet or muddy conditions.

Chapter 9
Finishing and final build

Once you've completed your Buggy and all the components have been fitted, with everything as you want it and all the welding finished, it's unfortunately time to take it all apart again in order to paint it – but I bet you won't be able to resist giving it a try before you do!

Label everything as you take it off, despite the fact that having built your Buggy you will know it very well – it's surprising how quickly you can forget, and how many of the nuts and bolts can be mixed up. Take care when draining and refilling the brake hydraulic system, and also if you need to drain the petrol tank or fuel line. Always use new brake fluid of the correct specification and avoid contact with the Buggy frame or your skin, as it can damage both. Please dispose of old fluid correctly, do not tip it down the drain.

PAINTING

Whichever method of finishing you intend to use, it's important that all the components are clean, de-greased and that any rust is removed with a wire brush and abrasive paper.

On my Buggy I had the frame

Fig. 9.1. The completed buggy assembled, but unpainted. (Steve Williams)

81

Fig. 9.2. A final check to make sure everything is in the right place. It's better to make any changes now rather than to have to do more drilling and welding after your Buggy has been finished. (Steve Williams)

Fig. 9.3. Unfortunately the temptation to give it a go (just to make sure it all works properly) is too great. This driver has let his enthusiasm get the better of him. Where's your crash helmet mate? (Steve Williams)

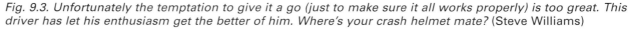

Fig. 9.4. The finished frame looks really smart ready to have everything bolted back into position. This one has been powder coated. (Steve Williams)

Fig. 9.5. Special metal paints can provide an easy-to-apply, durable finish. Some can be put straight on to metal, even rusty metal once the worst rust has been removed. (Steve Williams)

powder coated at a cost of £25 by a local powder-coating company, although (as you might have guessed) I had no choice of colour. To get a good price the frame went through the coating plant with another batch of components, so that's the colour I got!

A cheaper method of finishing would be to brush paint with a hard-wearing outdoor paint such as Hammerite, or spray with automotive paint which is available in aerosols.

It may be possible to take your completed frame and other parts to you local vehicle body shop for them to spray. Again, you may find it cheaper if they spray your frame with what is left in the spray gun at the end of another job.

You may find that items such as the pedals, rear axle and front stub axles, etc, get chipped and damaged if painted. You may prefer to get them zinc, cadmium or chrome plated. While this will add to the cost, it is likely to provide a more durable finish. On my Buggy I had these parts cadmium plated, and they certainly looked very good, creating a contrast with the painted frame.

Once your frame has been completed and painted, you'll find that the front and rear chassis tubes have open ends, which should be sealed against water and dirt entry using rubber or plastic bungs. This is important to guard against the risk of corrosion.

Fig. 9.6. We had parts that were likely to get chipped and damaged cadmium plated. (Steve Williams)

Fig. 9.7. Make sure that the self-locking nuts on the steering pivot bolts are correctly tightened, and lubricate the bolt threads. (Steve Williams)

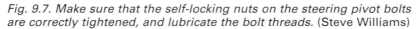

FINAL BUILD

As you finally put your finished Buggy back together again, make sure that all the bolts that need to be tight are, and check that items such as the rear axle, front axle assemblies, pedals, gear change and steering are all free to move as required. Grease all the pivot points and moving parts, and it's advisable to apply a small amount of general grease to all screw threads to help prevent them from rusting and seizing up.

When assembling the front hub carriers to the frame, it's important to make sure that the self-locking nuts on the steering pivot bolts are correctly tightened. If the nuts are too tight, the hub carriers will not be able to pivot and you'll have no steering, and if the bolts are too loose, there will be excessive play in the steering. Use copper grease or anti-seize compound to lubricate the bolt threads, and always renew

Fig. 9.8. The completed Buggy, ready to go! (Steve Williams)

the Nyloc nuts once they've been removed.

Remember to bleed the brake hydraulic system to remove the air before you use the Buggy (see Chapter 8), and also reconnect the gear-change mechanism, checking that it works correctly and that all gears can be selected. Adjust the gear-change linkage if necessary – see Chapter 8.

Finally, make sure that the chain is correctly tensioned, and reconnect the control cables, adjusting them until you're happy with the operation of all the controls. Lubricate the control pivots and the cables.

Chapter 10

Using your Buggy

So, now you've finished all the hard work involved in building your Buggy, you'll want to rush out and try it! But, before you do, there are a few things to bear in mind. Remember that your Buggy is not designed for use on the road, and indeed it would be illegal to do so – this means that you need to find somewhere safe to use your Buggy, ideally somewhere where you will not annoy other people! This Chapter provides advice on how to use your Buggy safely, and how to make sure that it stays in tip-top condition to provide you with many hours of fun.

FINDING SOMEWHERE TO USE YOUR BUGGY

Neither the author nor the publishers intend this Buggy to be used on a public highway. It does not comply with the Vehicle Construction and Use regulations in the UK. The Buggy is intended for off-road use on private property only.

First of all, you need to find somewhere to use your Buggy. The most important thing to remember here is that you must ask for and receive the landowner's permission before using your Buggy on any land which you don't own yourself. The chances are that if you explain exactly what you want to do, and

Fig. 10.1 Your Buggy should provide you with hours of fun, but always wear a helmet and suitable protective clothing. (Steve Williams)

show the person concerned your Buggy (perhaps even let them have a go behind the wheel), you'll find a sympathetic local landowner who will allow you to use your Buggy on his or her land. Remember that the Buggy, and especially its steering system, are designed to be used off-road, and if it's used on tarmac, tyre wear will be heavy, and you may find that the steering appears rather sluggish.

It goes without saying that wherever you use your Buggy, you must treat the land with respect, and if you're on a farm, or in open countryside, you should follow the country code.

Motor vehicles off-road

The Countryside and Rights of Way act 2000 makes it clear that driving any motor vehicle, including motor bikes, quad bikes and scrambler bikes (and, therefore a Buggy), on footpaths, bridleways, restricted byways or off-road is an offence, unless the driver has lawful authority.

The Country Code

● Enjoy the countryside and respect its life and work.
● Guard against all risk of fire.
● Fasten all gates.
● Keep your dogs under control.
● Keep to public paths across farmland.
● Use gates and stiles to cross fences, hedges and walls.
● Leave livestock, crops and machinery alone.
● Take your litter home.
● Help to keep all water clean.
● Protect wildlife, plants and trees.
● Take special care on country roads.
● Make no unnecessary noise.

INSURANCE

There is no legal requirement for the Buggy to be insured, but it would be worth checking with your insurance broker to see if you're covered on your existing household or motor policy for any 3rd party claims against you for injury or damage. If not, they will probably be able to arrange cover for you.

SAFETY WHEN USING THE BUGGY

When using the Buggy, safety must always be the first consideration. Be sensible, and always wear a crash helmet and suitable protective clothing. Above all, use common sense.

Helmet and clothing

A crash helmet should be worn at all times, and a suitable one can be purchased from a motorcycle accessory shop. Buy the best you can afford.

At all times wear adequate protective clothing, such as a one-piece overall. Never wear loose or trailing clothing, such as a scarf, which could get caught up in the wheels or drivetrain.

Seat

Make sure that your seat is securely fitted to the frame, whether it's a proper go-kart seat or whether you have used a plastic stacking-chair seat.

Seat belts

Whilst seat belts are not a legal requirement for an off-road Buggy, you may decide that it makes sense to fit them. I haven't used them because I feel that it's safer not to.

If you want to fit seat belts, consult an engineer about mountings etc, and use the appropriate bolts, washers, brackets and fixings. It's vital to make sure that the seat belt mountings are strong enough to cope with the loads they might have to handle – bear in mind that in cars, the seat belt mountings are bolted to special steel reinforcing plates. Always follow the manufacturer's advice when fitting seat belts.

Filling the Buggy with fuel

Do not smoke anywhere near an area where petrol is stored. Do not fill the Buggy's fuel tank when the engine it hot, and always stop the engine before filling with fuel.

Driving the Buggy

Although the Buggy is designed to be used off-road, bear in mind that it has no suspension, and it's not therefore suitable for use on rocky or boulder-strewn terrain. The ideal ground on which to use the Buggy is an open field with short grass, or a reasonably flat track. If you decide to drive the Buggy through long grass or vegetation, be prepared for any nasty surprises which may be hidden from view, such as large stones or tree-stumps.

When driving the Buggy up a steep incline, use low revs – this will reduce any risk of the Buggy tipping over backwards.

If you think that the Buggy is going to tip over, keep your hands on the steering wheel. As an additional safety feature, netting could be fitted to the Buggy frame to keep the driver's limbs and head within the frame – this will help to guard against injury if the Buggy tips over.

When using the brakes, remember that if you're driving off-

Fig. 10.2. If you're driving through long grass, beware of any nasty surprises which may be hidden from view. (Steve Williams)

road on grass, particularly wet grass, or mud, it will be very easy to lock-up the back wheels – the trick is to apply the brakes gently. This shouldn't prove to be a problem, in fact it will probably add to the fun, unless you're travelling towards something solid at the time!

Moving a Buggy which is stuck

The Buggy is quite light and can be picked up by two fit adults. In the unlikely event of the Buggy becoming stuck in mud, it can be lifted clear, but if resorting to towing, ensure that the tow rope is attached to a substantial part of the frame.

MAINTENANCE

To keep you Buggy in tip-top condition, and to make sure that it's safe, regular maintenance checks should be carried out both before and after use.

Before using the Buggy

● Check for fuel leaks.
● Check that the wheels are securely fastened.
● Check that the brake, accelerator and clutch cables are securely connected and that the linkages work.
● Check that the steering pivot pins are tightened correctly, and check the operation of the steering.
● Check the condition of the chain.
● Check the engine/gearbox oil level.

● Check the tyre pressures (where applicable).

After using the Buggy

● Clean the Buggy, paying particular attention to all the moving parts, such as the bearings, rear axle, control cables, chain, etc.
● Check the tightness of all fastenings.
● Where applicable, check the front wheel retaining split-pins and their washers for wear and damage.
● Lubricate the chain.
● Lubricate the steering pivot pins.

Finally, take care and have fun using your Buggy.

A happy customer – Derek Manders's granddaughter Charlotte tries out her new Buggy, . . .

. . . followed by Derek himself. (Steve Williams)

It looks as if this driver means business! (Steve Williams)

This is one of the buggies that took part in the inaugural University Air Squadron (UAS) Buggy Challenge at Abingdon in the summer of 2003. (James Coleman)

Another variation on the theme, also seen at Abingdon. Note the additional safety features – the extra roll-hoop on the front chassis tube and the plastic netting across the sides of the frame. (James Coleman)

This Buggy is built from square-section tube, and sports side-impact protection bars between the front and rear wheels. These bars were fitted to all the Buggies in the UAS Buggy Challenge – a wise precaution when sharing the track with other competitors. (James Coleman)

Appendix 1

Templates for fish-mouthing tubes

The following templates can be used as patterns for fish-mouthing tubes using 'The toilet roll trick' described in Chapter 4.

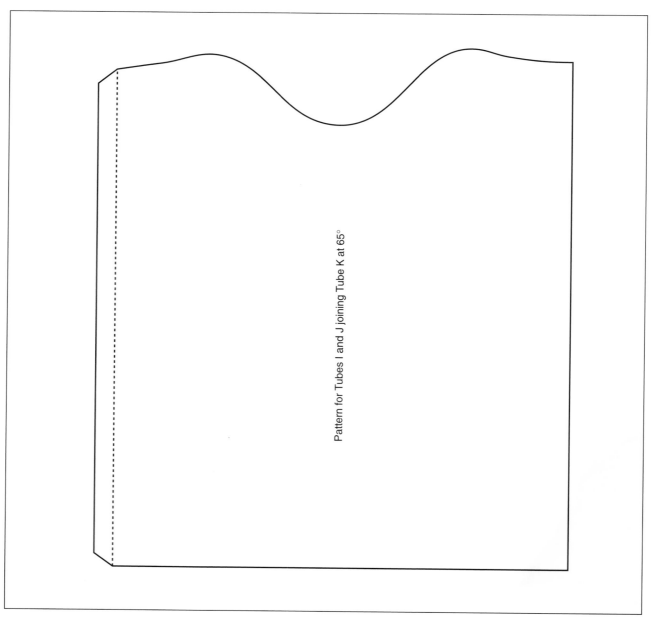

Pattern for Tubes I and J joining Tube K at 65°

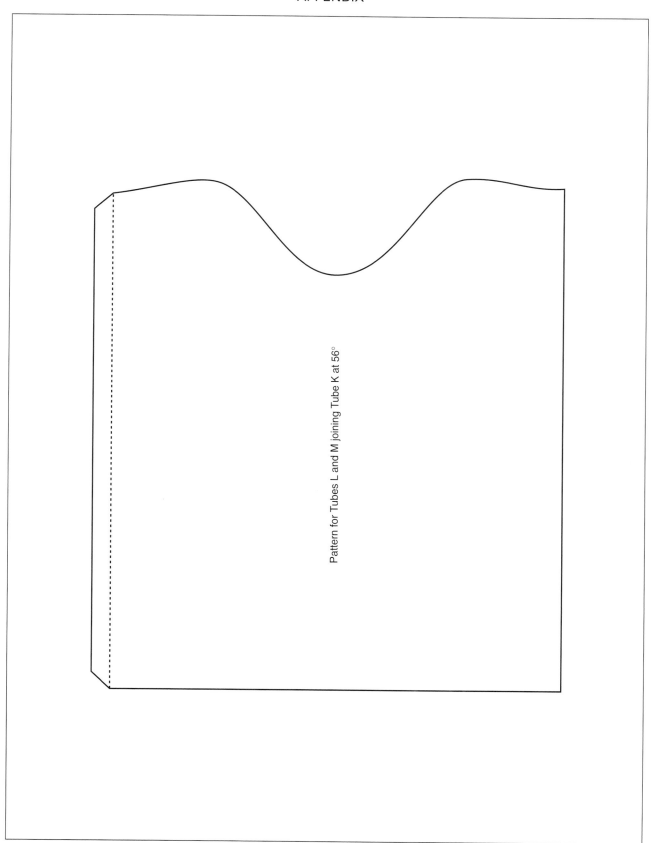

Pattern for Tubes L and M joining Tube K at 56°

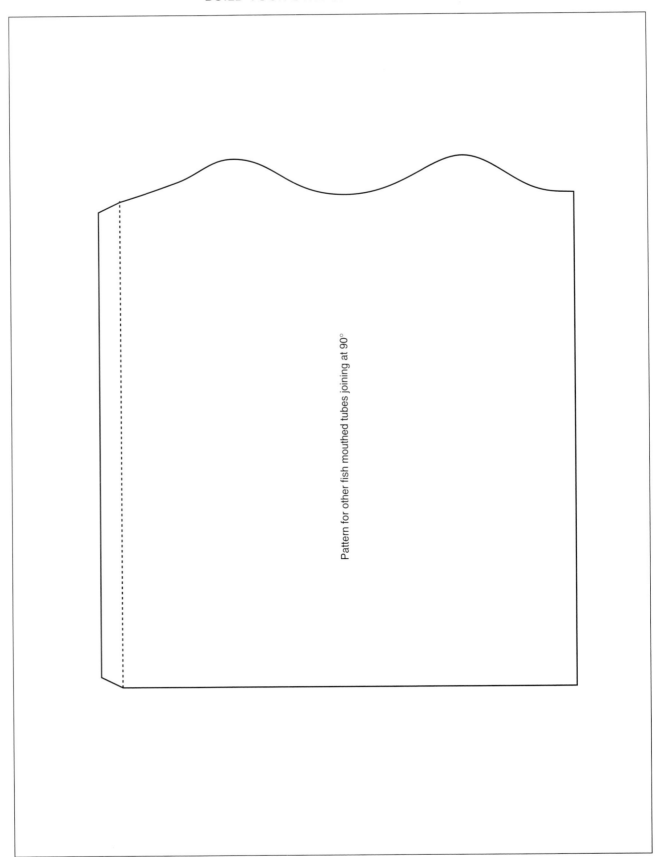

Pattern for other fish mouthed tubes joining at 90°

Other books from Haynes Publishing

Build Your Own Sports Car for as little as £250 – and race it!
by Ron Champion
ISBN 1 85960 636 9

Honda C50, C70 & C90 Service and Repair Manual
1967 to 1999
ISBN 1 85960 559 1

Car Builder's Manual
by Lionel Baxter
ISBN 1 85960 646 6

Automotive Welding Manual
The complete step-by-step guide to understanding, buying and using welding and cutting equipment
ISBN 1 85960 201 0

Motorcycle Basics TechBook (2nd Edition)
An overview of motorcycles and how they work
ISBN 1 85960 515 X

Motorcycle Workshop Practice TechBook (2nd Edition)
Essential information on how to use tools, fabricate components from metal and plastic, and tackle common motorcycle repairs
ISBN 1 85960 470 6

Motorcycle Fuel Systems TechBook
All carburettor types, along with fuel injection, from the basic theory to practical tuning
ISBN 1 85960 514 1

Race and Rally Car Source Book (4th Edition)
The guide to building or modifying a competition car
by Allan Staniforth
ISBN 1 85960 846 9

Competition Car Suspension (3rd Edition)
Design, construction, tuning
by Allan Staniforth
ISBN 1 85960 644 X

Competition Car Preparation
A practical handbook
by Simon McBeath
ISBN 1 85960 609 1

The Off-Road 4-Wheel-Drive Book (4th Edition)
Choosing, using and maintaining go-anywhere vehicles
by Jack Jackson
ISBN 1 85960 606 7

Repairing and Restoring Classic Car Components
by Peter and John Wallage
ISBN 1 85960 694 6

Two-Stroke Performance Tuning (2nd Edition)
by A. Graham Bell
ISBN 1 85960 619 9

Four-Stroke Performance Tuning (2nd Edition)
by A. Graham Bell
ISBN 1 85960 435 8

Modern Engine Tuning
By A. Graham Bell
ISBN 1 85960 866 3

For more information please contact:
Customer Services Department,
Haynes Publishing,
Sparkford, Yeovil, Somerset BA22 7JJ, England

Tel: 01963 442030 Fax: 01963 440001
Int. tel: +44 1963 442030
Int. Fax: +44 1963 440001

E-mail: sales@haynes.co.uk
Web site: www.haynes.co.uk